A GUIDE TO THE STUDY OF MANITOBA LOCAL HISTORY

GERALD FRIESEN and BARRY POTYONDI

A Guide to the Study of
Manitoba Local History

PUBLISHED BY THE UNIVERSITY OF MANITOBA PRESS
FOR THE MANITOBA HISTORICAL SOCIETY

This volume has been published with the assistance of the Manitoba Historical
Society, especially the H. Clare Pentland Memorial Fund, and the Government of
Manitoba.

Canadian Cataloguing in Publication Data

Friesen, Gerald, 1943-
    A guide to the study of Manitoba local
history

    Bibliography: p.
    ISBN 0-88755-121-1 bd.
    ISBN 0-88755-605-1 pa.

1. Manitoba — History, Local — Historiography.
2. Local history. I. Potyondi, Barry, 1954-
    II. Title
    FC3359.5.F75   971.27'007'2   C80-091061-3
    F1063.F75

Contents

Acknowledgments

This guide book owes its existence to Professor Ed Rea, former chairman of the Historic Sites Board of Manitoba, who suggested a paper on local history that I had presented to a community group be converted into a booklet. With the aid of John McFarland, director of the Historic Resources Branch, Government of Manitoba, I then embarked on the usual odyssey to find help and information. Three University of Manitoba students on summer employment grants, Robert Doyle, Donald Loveridge, and Eleanor Stardom, contributed material for the Appendices. Barry Potyondi, also a University of Manitoba student on a government grant, spent one full summer and much of his spare time in the following months preparing drafts for the text and bibliographies. His work forms an integral part of the final product and, because it is impossible to separate his contribution from mine, we have published the work under our joint authorship.

The basic material was completed in the autumn of 1977 but, as our project grew larger, the plans of the government began to change. The result was a hiatus of three years during which time I added new material and the staff at the Historic Resources Branch, particularly John McFarland and Donna Dul, canvassed alternatives for publication. We are grateful to the Manitoba Historical Society, and especially the H. Clare Pentland Memorial Fund, as well as to the Government of Manitoba, for the assistance which made possible the publication of this guide.

Many of our friends read portions of the manuscript and contributed material. We would like to thank Fred McGuinness, J.E. Rea, Ian Kerr, Jean Friesen, and W.L. Morton for reading and commenting upon the text; Jaye Fredrickson, Ken Osborne, Keith Wilson, John Ingram, Orysia Luchak, Wayne Moodie, and Barry Kaye for their comments upon particular sections where our own experience was slight; Alan Artibise and Mary Fredrickson for permission to reprint material; and the staff of the Provincial Archives and Legislative Library of Manitoba, for their generous and kind assistance on innumerable occasions and particularly Elizabeth Blight, who arranged for the illustrations. Donald Loveridge was a part of the project from its inception and deserves special thanks for his contribution. And so too does Patricia Lagacé who shepherded the manuscript through the University of Manitoba Press with efficiency and good humour.

A guide which encompasses so many topics will inevitably contain errors but we hope that they are few and that you, the reader, will let us know about our mistakes in order that they can be corrected. Most of all, we hope that the book will stimulate your interest in your community and encourage your historical studies.

Gerald Friesen
Barry Potyondi

A stagecoach on the Canadian prairies, late nineteenth century (courtesy Public Archives of Canada)

EMERSON, THE GATEWAY CITY ON THE RED RIVER.

Emerson, Manitoba, about 1880 (courtesy Public Archives of Manitoba)

Cotton Farm, Swan River District, Manitoba (courtesy Public Archives of Manitoba)

Christmas dinner at T. A. Kitts, 1908 (courtesy Public Archives of Manitoba)

Bar, 1912 (courtesy Public Archives of Manitoba)

Children from Dominion City Reserve at a picnic near Letellier, 1937 (courtesy Public Archives of Manitoba)

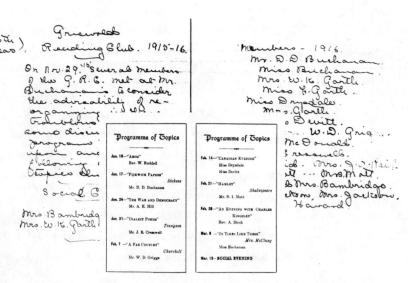

(16th year) Griswold Reading Club. 1915-16.

On Nov. 29.ᵗ ... several members of the G.R.C. met at Mr. Buchanan's to consider the advisability of re-organizing ...

... some discussion ... programme ... following ... topics ...

Social C ...

Mrs. Bambridge
Mrs. W. K. Garth

Programme of Topics

Jan. 10—"Amos"
Rev. W. Ruddell

Jan. 17—"Pickwick Papers"
Dickens
Mr. D. D. Buchanan

Jan. 24—"The War and Democracy"
Mr. A. E. Hill

Jan. 31—"Dialect Poems"
Tennyson
Mr. J. R. Creswell

Feb. 7 —"A Far Country"
Churchill
Mr. W. D. Griggs

Programme of Topics

Feb. 14—"Canadian Evening"
Miss Drysdale
Miss Devitt

Feb. 21—"Hamlet"
Shakespeare
Mr. S. I. Mott

Feb. 28—"An Evening with Charles Kingsley"
Rev. A. Birch

Mar. 6 —"In Times Like These"
Mrs. McClung
Miss Buchanan

Mar. 13—SOCIAL EVENING

Members - 1916.
Mr. D. D. Buchanan.
Miss Buchanan.
Mrs. W. K. Garth.
Miss L. Garth.
Miss Drysdale
Mrs. Garth.
... Devitt.
... W. D. Grig...
McDonald.
... Creswell.
... Mrs. ...
... Mrs. Mott.
& Mrs. Bambridge
... Mrs. Jackson
Howard

Griswold Reading Club Minute Book, 1915-16 (courtesy Public Archives of Manitoba)

Dec 19th   *Trustees*   Meeting Held in School House

P Jeffrey

C Garlick That we get the usual for Conas Bags ~~carried~~
       The organ being out of ~~order~~ repair, it was decided
       that we get Prof Fenwick out to fise it up,
       which was done at the cost of Seven dollars.

June 24 + 26 Trustees' &

       Meeting held in school house to discuss
       painting stable and outbuilding, and to put
       a gate in the west fence, and also to confirm
       the Sec action in retaining the present Teacher
       which was unanimous,

Moved by J Cofse

Sec   C Garlick that we retain the present teacher and
       raise the salary, 5 dollars per month.   Carried

Mov Mr Jeffrey

       Mr Garlick That we paint stable and outbuildng
       the color be red with white trim and that
       we all come if possible to put it on, and
       to erect swings and other repair work which
       is ne~~cces~~cessary,   Carried

Boss Hill School District 430, Minute Book, 19 December 1925 (courtesy Public Archives of Manitoba)

A GUIDE TO THE STUDY OF MANITOBA LOCAL HISTORY

CHAPTER 1

Introduction

We all play a game called "Do you remember?" from time to time. We ask someone to recall a familiar event and, as the words build a well-known picture, we sink back in our seats, the better to review sounds and shapes that compose the story of someone's first steps, or an old uncle's hearing aid, or the awesome blizzard. The game can have any number of players, any number of topics, and can last all evening, given such conditions as eager listeners, willing talkers, easy chairs and time to spare. How did you meet father? Why did grandmother travel west? Why did you settle down here? What happened to old Mr. Doe? It's a game of families and friends, a mixture of fact and fancy and pure tall tale, and it is fun. But what happens when a cool voice interjects at a special moment in the story of great grandmother's courtship: "That's absolute rubbish — it never happened that way at all. Why, I remember that old livery stable across from the station, and they couldn't have met there. It was torn down during the war when people started to drive cars. No, I know for a fact they met at a church social." And the debate heats up. When did the Great War start? Where was great grandmother's house? Who had the first car? Was it at the social that grandmother first met grandfather? The talk may ramble across the history of modern Europe before it settles down to another tale, but, as it does, our place in the family, the community and the nation has been established a little more clearly. We have had another lesson in who we are and where we come from.

Local history fixes our place in the world in just the same fashion as the fireside game of "Do you remember?" It takes immediate topics, subjects that are very close to each of us, and studies them thoroughly: three generations of one family, the first century of a local church, the story of a town and district. Individuals, institutions and communities are the focus of the work. Because the topics are close to us, they are the source of entertainment as well as instruction. We actually study ourselves and our homes.

This book is a guide to the study of local history in Manitoba. Because it stands alone in its field, it addresses readers whose needs differ greatly. The teacher in primary school wants projects for a grade six class; the teacher in high school is looking for manageable essay or research topics; the university student seeks help on a major term paper; and the local historical committee wishes to publish a volume on town and district for a centennial celebration. In order to meet each of these demands, this first chapter addresses three special needs — those of the local historian, the teacher, and the student — in three separate sections. The book then describes local history as a field for research in chapters two to fourteen; and finally in the appendices, it provides additional detail on the location and use of particularly valuable sources of information.

This is a guidebook and, like any other guide to the delights of a foreign land, it merely points the way to the reader. It suggests what topics should be studied, how to learn about these topics, and what questions might be answered in the course of the investigation. It is not the only book you will need. Whether you are a teacher, student, or local historian, you will find specialized books to assist you in adapting this information, which concerns only Manitoba, to the needs of classroom, essay, or historical project. Many of these supplementary works are listed in the chapters which follow. This volume is not a history of local communities in Manitoba. Though it suggests how this history might appear, the guidebook can only point out lines of enquiry because, as yet, we know too little of our past to make final judgments. Not is it a provincial history. Several distinguished volumes do exist in this category, however, and you will find them to be indispensable in your study.

This guidebook may sustain another round of that family game "Do you remember?" but its major purpose is to assist Manitobans in their study of themselves and to aid them in establishing their place in the world.

TO LOCAL HISTORIANS IN MANITOBA

Local and family studies have become boom industries on the prairies in recent days and promise to retain their popularity for years to come. One result of this widespread interest has been a flood of enquiries to archives and historical societies about sources of information and methods of research. The following pages will answer some of your questions. Please do not be worried about the vast range of available sources; the book is intended to serve university classes as well, and thus covers ground that may interest only the specialist.

Citizens interested in the history of a community have two obligations: preservation and education. Preservation of historical records can be undertaken with the help of local history teachers and librarians, and of the archivists at the Provincial Archives of Manitoba or the Rural Archives of Brandon University. In either case, the archives will preserve and organize the material so that it will be available to future generations and will ensure that copies are made for deposit in a local school or public facility. Rather than accept the destruction of precious historical documents, which has happened too often in recent times, the local committee can ensure that town records, school board minutes, church registers, private diaries, club scrapbooks, photographs, and letters become a part of our community heritage.

Education, or maintaining local awareness of community history, can be accomplished by many effective and inexpensive means. Consider some of the following alternatives. If you wish to prepare a biographical record of your district, the main component of many local histories, use a biographical questionnaire and publish a "mug-book." If there is widespread interest in your district, ask for copies of photographs of family members and sell subscriptions to your publication. If this is too ambitious, simply mimeograph resulting family histories for local distribution, and do remember to place copies in the Legislative Library and Archives.

If your goal is the preservation of historical records in your area, consider the establishment of a local repository in a centrally located public, community college, or high school library. There is little point in publishing this documentary material, but do preserve it. Students will derive much pleasure and benefit from a collection of photographs, letters, and other documents concerning the history of their district.

You may want to prepare an essay or a series of articles on aspects of local history for publication in a local newspaper or in some other journal. The following chapters will suggest some topics and sources; other approaches, including biographies and special events, will also be obvious. When completed and published, these papers should also be placed in the archives and in the local historical collection for future use.

Another pleasant project of this type is the preparation of one of several varieties of brief illustrated history of the district. The more ambitious format is a forty or fifty-page booklet containing an average of one or two pictures per page and about three to five thousand words of text. Since space is limited, these booklets address only a limited number of questions, among which may be choice of townsite, changes in population and ethnic or religious patterns, economic functions, principal social institutions, and the role of a few leading citizens.

A variation on this format which is more flexible and often more entertaining for the historical committee and audience alike is the preparation of slide shows, with typed, taped, or "live" commentary. Here, the format requires a short text and appropriate slides (thirty to fifty slides, with commentary, result in a programme of forty-five minutes to an hour). Historic photographs, illustrations taken from books, paintings, cartoons, maps, local sites and buildings, local furniture and silverware and clothing, catalogue illustrations and a town dump, all can provide lively images to complement the lecture or commentary.

The common guidelines for these projects are clear: choose topics that are well defined and manageable; choose a format (booklet, slide show, mug-book), that is appropriate for the audience or consumer; include illustrations to make the story palatable to the casual passer-by; and distribute the product on an occasion that will ensure a good reception, such as an anniversary service or centenary celebration.

You need not publish a line to establish a sense of continuity between past and present in your community. It takes only a little research to draft a few lines for plaques, whether of bronze, ceramic tile or wood, to commemorate important buildings, events, sites, and individuals. Similarly, place names, whether of streets or buildings, can preserve the memory of historic events. Preservation of historic sites and buildings is now regarded as an important activity and should be one concern of every local history committee.

Local committees usually begin because the town or district wants to celebrate a special event like the centenary of British or European settlement. Local pride demands a monument to pioneer achievements; there is a fear that the stories of early days are in danger of being lost forever; residents want to understand their place in district and province and country; school children are to learn about their roots — whatever the original impetus, a committee is formed, the museum is founded, and the next project is inevitably a book. Before you get carried away, please pause and consider the following ideas and advice.

Working with local history is a pleasure. It is familiar and yet distant, challenging and yet easy, and above all it is a valuable contribution to your community and to your grandchildren. Local history is growing in popularity; by embarking on any type of historical project, you are likely to find dozens of kindred spirits at similar meetings in the coming years. But what type of project do you undertake? That is an important and even delicate matter, upon which we can offer only our own experience.

The traditional prairie response to the demand for a "local history" has been the preparation of a book or booklet which attempted to discuss the entire history of a community. In the last thirty years, as many as four or five thousand local studies may have appeared, though it is difficult to be certain because many have since vanished. What are these works like? They contain an odd assortment of pieces of information: biographical sketches of pioneers; lists or maps of early landowners; descriptions of early businesses and transportation systems; stories of ball teams, curling rinks, church construction and school concerts; lists of firsts (as in first telephone, car, radio), and of unusual events such as hail storms, blizzards, murders, fires, and so on. Are the books useful? The answer is both yes and no. The books are valuable because they record information that is unavailable and may never be recovered. Interviews with early citizens, information from former residents who can no longer be traced, photographs which have since been destroyed — these are the items that give early local history its worth. The books are inadequate, on the other hand, because they are poorly written, impossible to follow from beginning to end, factually unreliable, and do not contain an index or even, in many cases, maps.

In sum, the books preserve the historical record but they do not interpret the community to outsiders in a striking or meaningful fashion. Many of you will recognize the sensation of trying to read another district history and becoming bogged down in unfamiliar events and meaningless names. There seems to be no story to the narrative. We often leave these books with the feeling that we still do not understand the real spirit of a community or the important influences that shaped it. And yet, despite our disappointment, we are happy that the stories have been saved. The book may be inadequate but its collection of documents is invaluable.

These times are past. We believe that you, members of the local historical committee, should free yourselves from the chains of book-making and re-think the reasons for your committee's existence. Surely the great contribution of the earlier committees was not the publication of their work in book form but the preservation of historical records and the public historical education that were byproducts of the labour.

If you remain convinced that a one-volume history should be written, please investigate the avenues of research mentioned in the following chapters, consider the suggestions to teachers in the following section, and turn to chapter 14 on book publishing. Whatever your choice, welcome to the study of local history. May you find it challenging and rewarding.

TO THE TEACHER

You are bombarded with bright ideas about raising the level of your performance at every in-service and extension meeting you attend, so the prospect of yet more advice will be daunting. As a consequence, we begin with a word of caution: this book is not an urgent campaign on behalf of a dazzling new product; rather, it is a guide to make your work easier if you have decided to make local studies part of your classroom activity. Aside from listing sources of information and types of assignment, it will not provide short-cuts or serve as a last-minute lesson aid. As usual, you will do most of the work. Having said that however, we will acknowledge our conviction that local history is an excellent means to introduce the study of the past.

Many exhortations about local studies have been published in recent years, so a review of the arguments in favour of local history in the classroom can be brief. The most obvious, of course, is that it gives students an introduction to history itself, and thus access to the common culture of the community. It also aids their appreciation of contemporary society by demonstrating the many facets of a community and how such activities and groups have developed over a long period. By selecting individuals for special attention, too, local history aids students' comprehension of human motivation and relationships and the very process of maturation and aging. But if these virtues might be attributed to all historical study, the special strength of local history is the sense of immediacy and "real life" which it evokes in many students. By studying their own locale in depth, students can experience the gap in time between their age and others without also having to make an imaginative leap into another and undoubtedly less familiar place. The subject lends itself to interdisciplinary approaches because mathematics, geography, social science, even biology and domestic arts can be applied to local study. And "history" itself can seem more alive when not only textbooks but building facades and grandparents and cemeteries and business directories become sources for research.

One important reason for studying history, aside from the patriotic or moral lessons it provides, is the development of certain intellectual skills. At the simplest level, which begins in our early years, history requires the skill of comprehension, the ability to understand the content of a message or unit of study. It then requires translation, the ability to take information in one form (a table on population, for example), and present it in another form (a graph or a paragraph), in order to explain its salient features. From there, historical study develops the ability to analyse, which is defined as recognizing differences or similarities between two or more sources of information, recognizing the significance of bias or perspective in these sources, and estimating the relative merits of these different accounts. Finally, it teaches the student how to create a synthesis; that is, to select material from a variety of sources on a given theme and to communicate it to others in an effective form. Such a list of skills will seem to be nothing more than the old virtues of critical reading and fluent writing, but these categories do define the requirements of curricula. The topics should require the comprehension of a body of facts (the level of complexity of which should be determined by the level of the class), the presentation of these facts in different forms, the ability to distinguish between and evaluate various sources of information, the obligation to reach conclusions about the topic, and the compilation of the results in a coherent fashion.

Having listed the advantages of the study of local history, we should mention some of the obvious pitfalls in using it as a school subject. Of these the worst is undoubtedly the danger of becoming an antiquarian. It is interesting to visit the graveyard in St. François-Xavier, entertaining to list nineteenth-century burials, noteworthy that Pascal Breland (a famous hunter and political leader) is interred beneath an attractive stone that might merit a photograph or rubbing. But once you have organized an outdoor education adventure for your group, what has been accomplished by the visit, the inventory of headstones, and the notice of the Breland marker? As historical study, absolutely nothing. Open-ended adventures of this sort must be converted into bits of information that fit a larger structure. In this case, Red River society, Metis economy, the West as a fur trade frontier, the eclipse of the Metis in a new Ontario-style Manitoba, all could be associated with a visit to St. François-Xavier. To put the illustration in broader terms, there should be reason for the study of each topic and for the adoption of projects or assignments; these reasons should be linked to the purpose of the course; and thus, in our opinion at least, a curriculum outline, whether locally or centrally created, is essential if antiquarianism is to be avoided in a local history course.

Aside from this one significant danger, the other pitfalls of local study will seem minor or at least trite. Some observers fear that students and teachers will become parochial in outlook if they gaze too long at their own community. And, of course, this is true. We must study other areas, and we must recognize that ours is not necessarily the most valuable or best or most important of places or lifestyles. Rather, it is one way, our own way, and we should try to understand it and appreciate it within a broader perspective.

Another criticism of local study concerns the student's product. Videotapes and cassettes and movies seem creative and innovative, but verbal and literary skills are still of paramount importance and should be a main point of the exercise. An illustrated essay or speech is still the best "medium" for communicating one's knowledge. The more complicated techniques too often consume valuable time in learning how to employ the hardware, or as it is now called, the software.

Finally, there are the inevitable problems for the teacher associated with the creation of a new course such as local history: we must define the topic and the boundaries of the subject carefully; we must enumerate the themes; and we must know how to find the answers to the problems of research. Teachers cannot rely upon the universities to present courses in their local areas, though a history of Winnipeg is now available and a general introduction to local study may soon be offered at the University of Manitoba. Rather, your own general reading in national and regional history will have to provide the foundation for the course. Once you have mastered a few of the standard works in regional and provincial history, such as those of W.L. Morton and G.F. Stanley, you might turn to previously published histories of your district to learn the basic outlines of your topic. At this point, you should also read the standard monographs on industries and other institutions or activities central to your region, such as V.C. Fowke's *National Policy and the Wheat Economy* or Frank H. Epp's *The Mennonites in Canada.* You are now ready to prepare two lists, one noting the important themes peculiar to the locality, such as Icelandic settlement or a unique railway builder, and another noting topics which your area shares with other districts in the region, such as the Depression and recent rural depopulation. The lists, like the readings, are essential preparation for the course. Without adequate knowledge of regional history, your detailed planning of class projects and the collection of source materials would be wasted.

As you will see from the following chapters, for even one small district the range of primary source materials is huge. The main categories include published sources, unpublished sources, and physical or material sources, such as buildings and furniture. The student and teacher alike might be attracted to the use of unpublished records (for example, political papers and town minutes), but they should beware of losing their way in the endless morass of records or of imitating the often-deadening routine of original research that is required of a professional historian. There is sufficient material in published and government records to keep most school classes occupied in useful and interesting assignments. Do remember that the point of the local history course is to stimulate enquiry and explanation by means of immediate examples rather than to write a new local history. Published documents are available from the Hudson's Bay Record Society (dealing largely with fur trade records), the Manitoba Record Society, and a number of government departments. Additional material appears in map and photographic archives and in newspaper files.

Once the material has been consulted, you must choose between two approaches to the course: 1) Structured units: By choosing a specific theme, you can select in advance the illustrative documents, duplicate them for ready consultation, and exercise almost complete control over the student project, thus ensuring that the documentary material will be varied in type and not too lengthy. This approach obviously restricts the students' experience of "history-writing" but it ensures that the results of their labours will have some relationship to the course. 2) Data-bank or mini-archive: By choosing to create a research facility at a central place in the district, the teacher can assemble a wide range of resource materials for use by students and others for many years to come, but this approach poses its own problems. The ideal archive would contain a complete census record for the district; copies of as many topographical, geological, soil and transportation route maps as can be found (including especially the two atlases of Manitoba); the poll-by-poll election results and descriptions of poll boundaries for every election; climate records; the township plans and sectional maps for the district; insurance plans of the town; field crop and farm income records; excerpts from directories such as those compiled by Henderson and, where available, Dun and Bradstreet; copies of company registration records and annual reports; a slide and photograph collection; excerpts from relevant statistics and reports prepared by government agencies, such as the reports of the Education Department, the Indian Affairs Department, the school inspector, the Agriculture Department; lists of those who have held professional and official posts in the district, including council members, nurses, doctors, teachers, judges, and so on; finally, and most important of all, the local newspaper. Microfilm copies of many local papers have been prepared, so the basic work has been done, but a microfilm reader (costing approximately $1000) and the film itself would have to be purchased. The newspapers at the Provincial Library can be borrowed by inter-library loan or purchased at a cost of about $20 per reel if they are not already available at the local library or newspaper office. (A weekly paper of reasonable size will be filmed at the rate of about two years or thirty months per reel.)

The creation of an archive of this magnitude is a considerable task but not a forbidding one. A few months, spread over several summers, for example, will produce an invaluable resource that can be used with profit for years to come. The archive might cost several thousand dollars, including the purchase of a microfilm reader and the allocation of twenty or thirty feet of shelf space, a photographic and slide file, and several larger drawers for map storage. And it would probably lead to the purchase of a number of books for the library: the bibliography in this volume will provide some suggestions and indicate the number of obvious works which should be available. But this is far beyond the requirements of the primary or secondary school system in any district and should be undertaken only if an active historical committee is prepared to accept the responsibility for initial cost and upkeep. The point of the exercise, after all, is to collect materials that can be adapted to the needs of various classes and individuals by numerous teachers. And, however rich the local resource collection becomes, the foundation of the local history class will still lie in the library (that is, in secondary studies of the field), and in the assistance provided by the teacher to the student.

And what will the local history class do? Let us assume that you have already acquired considerable expertise in regional studies through university courses and independent reading and that you have begun to collect local source materials. Your concern is now for workable projects and assignments. First, let's deal with primary classes, since grade six has become a focus for local history in Manitoba. If your first goal is to establish a sense of chronology or a feel for "time past," one convenient approach is through family history. *My Backyard History Book*, by David Weitzman, though thin gruel at the best of times, gives half its pages to varieties of family projects: family tree, map, portrait, recipe collection, archive of photographs, migration or travel, pets, cars, school days, babies, soldiers, athletes, and houses.

A second goal is to establish other links with the past through the study of family names and place names. To be effective, this analysis should be extended to the earliest possible roots and, thus, the origin of Wolseley School might be traced not only to Sir Garnet Wolseley, leader of the military expedition to Red River in 1870, but also the English origins of the Wolseley name.

A third popular introduction to the past is through material history — a study of the origin, use, and style of objects and buildings. A sad iron, a butter churn or mold, a kerosene lamp, a corset, and a quill pen can be useful historical sources and convenient routes of access to earlier generations. The questions that can be raised include not only what is this object, but when was it used, why was this particular type in use, who made it, did it belong to a particular social class or national group, or is there a significance to its style? Mary Fredrickson, a teacher who has had much success with this type of study in her Nova Scotia classrooms, tells the story of a sad iron which might have appeared in a farm dump:

Although the function of the sad iron is obvious, students should be encouraged to think about the task of ironing in a home without electricity. Mere lifting of the iron will indicate the physical stamina neded to iron the family's wash. The question of how the iron was heated may arise. The answer is that it was heated on a cast-iron wood stove. This, in turn, leads to consideration of the sad iron's history.

When this iron was first introduced in Atlantic Canada homes it was considered to be a marvelous labour-saving device. Until the latter half of the 19th century all but the wealthiest of homes were equipped with fireplaces for cooking and as a source of heat. Heating irons in the fireplace posed problems, one of which was the problem of keeping the iron clean. Students may guess that in the days before the cast iron stove, a hot iron bar or brick or even live coals were placed inside the huge, hollow earlier version of the iron. Only when the effects of the Industrial Revolution began to be felt was it possible to increase household efficiency — and reduce some of the time-consuming labour. In the Chignecto Isthmus area, the advent of the Intercolonial Railway and the establishment of foundries like Robb's in Amherst, N.S., or Fawcett's in Sackville, N.B., eventually brought the cast iron stove into the humblest kitchen. The sad iron soon followed.

At this point, the question of technology could be considered. "How was the iron manufactured?" A project on foundries is a possibility. Casting sad irons from molten iron was an important, if secondary, product of many of these foundries.

Other lines of inquiry are, of course, open for investigation. Sad irons, stoves and similar manufactured goods did save labour in the home. At the same time they created a dependency on industrialization and reduced the self-sufficiency of the family farm. Money had to be earned to buy items, which soon became necessities. Gradually, and relentlessly the concept of the farm changed, as did the roles of women, and the family unit itself. Students may wish to explore these changes under the general caption of "progress" and make comparisons between past and present events in this respect.

A grade six class can study "then and now" — the popular version of historical change — through the use of old and modern maps, directories, and fire insurance atlases. In Manitoba, where a rich collection of these records has been preserved in the Legislative Library and the Provincial Archives, the study of local topography, communications systems, businesses, and neighbourhoods is not only possible but easily arranged. Photographic collections and old buildings suggest studies of architectural style. Timetables and ticket prices in old directories encourage examination of comparative travel costs and times. Old catalogues permit comparative shopping and, with the use of the federal Department of Labour reports on the cost of living and wage levels, estimates on comparative standards of living. The construction of models of landscape (to rebuild Main Street, for example), the preparation of maps, the creation of graphs and tables, the establishment of photographic exhibits, all can supplement oral and written assignments.

Secondary school teachers face a more difficult problem because they often have less flexibility in the allocation of class time. Thus, the first decision for you to make is whether you wish to study local history in its own right, perhaps for one-quarter of the year's work, or whether you will employ it simply as an illustration of broader regional and national themes. The two approaches are quite different and will require rather different preparation.

If you plan to study local history in its own right, the introductions to chronology suggested for grade six — family, place name, and material history — are useful, if only as a means of establishing a sense of time and of personal involvement. The goal of the local history unit will be more advanced however, and will probably include appreciation of social differences (between ethnic groups, for example), economic function (why did this town develop in this place?), or the relationship between transportation technology, on the one hand, and economic change on the other (the transition from canoe to steamboat to railway). It might also focus upon education, religion, or leisure activities as a means of understanding ethnic and class differences, the variations in urban and rural life styles, and the social changes of the last century. The rhythms of local history can be described through the examples of Winnipeg and Minnedosa.

The first phase of local history in Manitoba might involve a study of the environment, and especially of the residue of the retreating glaciers, and of native peoples prior to European contact, that is before 1600 or 1650. The next phase would be the fur trade era or the period of native-white contact, from 1650 to about 1810, in the case of Winnipeg, or to 1870 in the case of Minnedosa. Next would be the age of transition from the interdependent economy of natives and whites to a society and economy governed by European and Canadian rules; in Red River, this occurred between 1810 and 1870, while in Minnedosa it took place during the 1870s. The establishment of the new society occurred very quickly in the Canadian West; in Winnipeg, one could say that the new order had imposed its impression upon landscape and mind between about 1870 and 1885, while in Minnedosa the process occurred between 1880 and about 1900. At this point, the stories diverge, as the following chapters will suggest, but certain clear similarities should be noted. The era to 1914 was, broadly speaking, a period of expansion and prosperity. The years from 1914 to the early 1920s saw unrest and instability and some social change. Modern communications, such as the car, the radio, the telephone, and where available, electric appliances, transformed life in the

1920s. The 1930s are properly described as the Depression decade. The Second World War and the decade that followed, through to 1956, saw provincial life change radically once again as thousands of rural dwellers left for the cities, and Winnipeg, in particular, grew dramatically. And the last two decades have seen the establishment of a kind of equilibrium in both rural and urban society, as changes in communications technology and in Manitoba's place in the world economy have not overturned her social arrangements. A similarly broad outline of local history in the province could be used as a model for course organization. The traditional approaches of lecture and assigned reading could be used to cover some segments of the story, and individual or small-group projects might focus on two or three other segments. The result would be a survey of the locality from early times to the present.

Which segments of local history, whether of Minnedosa or Winnipeg, best lend themselves to secondary school research projects? You will know the capacity of your students and their interests but we suggest that the 1870-1945 era should be the focus of class research because research materials are most readily available for that period. The likeliest themes include topography (the transition from an original physical to a man-made landscape), communications (from fur routes to railways to highways, or from mail to telegraph to radio, or even from the newspapers of 1860 to those of 1880 and 1920), economic change (in rural agricultural specialization or in Winnipeg's functions), general population characteristics of a census district (total, ethnicity, age composition, religion, occupation), and the nature and purpose of schooling. In each case, you will have to acquire specialized knowledge, and establish the research collection, before the project can begin. The following chapters are intended to lighten these tasks.

The second use of local history, as an illustration of national history, has often been a part of Manitoba teachers' programmes and therefore requires less comment. If the survey of Canadian history is discussing that famous example of staple economics, the fur trade, it is valuable to visit Lower Fort Garry or Fort Ellice or some other trade site. The Lower Fort is, of course, a particularly useful illustration of nineteenth-century fur trade society; it is a short step from the fur loft to European economic empires and a trading company's relationship with native peoples. The opening of the West, a crucial aspect of Confederation, can be analysed through population statistics — local, provincial, and national — and the uneasy French-English relationship can be canvassed in local newspaper columns, especially at the time of the schools questions (1890-6 and 1916), and conscription (1917). Depression and world war were local as well as national phenomena, of course, and so was the post-1945 flight to the cities. But these are just examples; local illustration of national themes has become commonplace in history courses, and such classroom aids as the slide sets in Canada's Visual History series make effective use of the approach.

TO THE UNIVERSITY STUDENT

You may eventually be a teacher of local history in the Manitoba school system, in which case the preceding pages will interest you, but for the moment you are approaching the topic as you would any other academic discipline. Local history is a topic just as worthy of analysis as the history of medieval England or macroeconomics but, because it has only recently attained such respectability, you will inevitably find a few who question its usefulness. The following pages address this problem of local history as a field of study.

History is concerned with the whole life of man in past society. As prairie students, you will have found, however, that the study of history involves governments and wars more often than local curling events and spring-tooth cultivators. The difference is usually explained by reference to the relative importance of the two spheres: the fate of nations, it is said, is much more significant than the fate of Birtle or Ste-Rose-du-Lac. No one would wish to question the importance of international affairs, but recognition of their influence should not belittle the significance of local events, which can be just as interesting, just as challenging as subjects of enquiry and, in their own way and proper place, just as worthy of attention as the story of the rise and fall of great civilizations.

You embark upon historical investigations in order to increase the breadth and depth of your understanding of the world and to refine your intellectual skills. As Professor G.R. Elton has suggested, the breadth will be supplied by new topics and unfamiliar experiences, but studies in depth are best undertaken in familiar areas. Work with primary sources, examination of historical controversies, and the marshalling of evidence to explain complex situations should be undertaken in a familiar language, cover familiar terrain, and be fitted into a longer period whose general outlines are clearly known. Nothing is more frustrating in one's early ventures into original research than the feeling that one has no solid ground, no sense of reality, no feel for events in the bewildering pages of documents from another era. (The sensation is acute enough when one is on familiar ground.) The history of Manitoba has been discussed clearly and thoroughly in a number of volumes; studies of particular themes provide background for most of the following chapters; the memories of parents and grandparents will introduce a society that is in many respects only a century old; and your own experience, because you have spent fifteen or twenty years in a community, will prompt valuable questions, suggest useful resource materials, and lead to interesting conclusions concerning the structure and working of the local society.

This is not to suggest that local history is a fit subject for a full programme in university. Professor Elton, whose opinions were mentioned in the above paragraph, was discussing a three or four-year history course in which the backbone, the compulsory subject, would be a study of familiar terrain — that is, a topic in one's national history — in great depth while optional courses provided the far-ranging experience that is also important. The study of Canadian history, in this view, would still be a requirement. While one of perhaps three to five courses in national history might be devoted to local topics, the great majority of time would be concerned with regional and national matters. Ideally too, the experience of writing history from local primary materials would be related to these broader themes.

To judge from the publications of the last half-century, local history has not been the subject of much professional interest in Canada. University scholars have been determined, it is true, to capture what is particular about the experience and the environment of the nation, as the descriptive passages in Donald Creighton's work and the extensive travels of Harold Adams Innis will attest. And it is also apparent that the fruitful contacts between scholars of the various disciplines in the social sciences and humanities have provided these historians with a broad understanding of social forces. But the concern for physical and economic analysis and the desire to provide a national history have resulted in a concentration on regional and national themes — constitutional autonomy, the staples trade, and regional protest movements, for example — rather than on local society. Though scholars in the associated disciplines have studied local topics, historical publications have only recently reflected a turn to this narrower field. A list of the professional historian's publications is not the only measure of his interest or of his scholarly activity, however, and the experience of the enthusiastic lay historian in every province during the twentieth century would contradict the accusation of professional neglect. Through historical societies, lecture engagements, editorial and archives boards, and historic sites committees, Canadian historians have been continually engaged in activities related to the study of local history. The state of Canadian historical thought and national perceptions, not the interests and activities of the historian, kept scholars from applying their full attention to a study of local society.

Changes in the perception of historical study, especially the increasing interest in social history as opposed to political history, and increasing attention to regional forces in Canada, along with the unprecedented growth of university history departments in the 1960s and early 1970s, have laid the foundations for greater scholarly attention to the history of smaller communities and of rural districts. The recent demand for Canadian content in the school curriculum and for student experience with primary sources in their history classes will ensure that local history also becomes a part of the high school and university programme.

One important aspect of this rise to respectability of "town pump gossip" (allegedly the predominant genre of local studies in earlier days) was the development of a Department of English Local History at the University of Leicester whose leaders have insisted upon "exact scholarship, wide sympathies, and a style of writing at once precise and vivid." The great achievement of these scholars has been to demonstrate that local history is a subject worthy of study in its own right. A historian of the Leicester school, H.P.R. Finberg, has argued that the study of the constituent parts of the nation do not "add up" to a history of the nation. Rather, local history is a topic different in nature from national history; it has its own themes, its own chronologies or periods, and, to a great extent, its own sources. Finberg has also asserted that the smaller unit is just as worthy of study as the larger, because the daily round of local activities — home and work, eating and sporting, seasonal rhythms, marriage and death — touch people in ways as significant as the rise and fall of nation-states. Another exponent of this viewpoint is Harold Perkin, who has called for the study of the district "society," seen as a "structured, functioning, evolving, self-regenerating, self-reacting whole, set in its geographical and cosmic environment." His description of the goal of social history — an understanding of people in their institutional setting — is thus another definition of the goal of local historical study.

If this English approach to local social studies has been one factor in the growing popularity of the field, another useful example can be found in the work of French historians who have developed somewhat different analyses to answer the same concerns. Lucien Febvre and Marc Bloch were the dominant figures in the development of a journal, *Annales: Economies, Sociétés, Civilisations,* and in the establishment of an approach to historical study that has been called the "Annales school." Its hallmark is at once precise attention to detailed study of the local environment and economy and concern for generalizations. Thus, analysis of climate and topography and seasonal migration of animal herds will be associated with the history of a province of France or even of the entire Mediterranean basin. In the introduction to his study of *The Mediterranean and the Mediterranean World in the Age of*

Philip II, Fernand Braudel defined the ideal of this historical approach: "Is it possible somehow to convey simultaneously both that conspicuous history which holds our attention by its continual and dramatic changes — and that other, submerged, history, almost silent and always discreet, virtually unsuspected either by its observers or its participants, which is little touched by the obstinate erosion of time? . . . Historians have over the years grown accustomed to describing this contradiction in terms of *structure* and *conjuncture*, the former denoting long-term, the latter, short-term realities." Thus, Braudel organized his book in three parts, the first dealing with the slow changes of man's relationship to his environment, the second with the rhythms of man's groupings — economic systems, states, societies, civilizations — and the third with traditional history, the story of individuals and events that he calls the crest on the tides of history. His work could be a model for any student of social history.

Of all the "national historiographies" which have influenced the Canadian historical discipline in recent years, none has been as influential as the American. Through graduate schools, personal contacts, and obvious historical parallels, the American innovations have had a great influence on the social sciences and humanities, including the study of social history. A survey of the literature on towns and families in New England alone, for example, provides numerous insights into social organization and suggests many questions to be asked in the Canadian context. Similarly, the developments in urban history, immigration history, women's history, business history, labour history and so on have been followed by Canadians and, where possible, or appropriate, have resulted in parallel studies in this country. Though one must be wary of the assumption that the two countries travel in tandem, one can learn much from the work of American historians.

The debt of this book to the various schools of social history will be readily apparent. The first and longest section, chapters two through eight, is devoted to a study of the "skeleton" of the local community. Here, one traces the patterns of similarity and difference between local districts by asking the same questions of the same series of sources. What is the influence of the environmental stage upon which the characters perform? Here topography, climate, drainage, soils and flora and fauna will be noted. What was the process of peopling this district? Factors that can be described by population statistics — arrivals, births and deaths, ethnicity and household size — will be discussed in this section. How did goods and people move within and beyond the boundaries of the region? Transportation and communications networks, fundamental sinews of the economy, are described here. In most parts of Manitoba, farming and other primary resource industries were the foundation of local economic activity, though most settlements also had small businesses. These activities are discussed under the headings of agriculture and business. Finally, the political structures are discussed. Every district can be examined under most of these headings. The student will seek to determine how his district compares with the rest and to discover wherein lies the distinctiveness of the local experience.

The work of Finberg and the Leicester school will be apparent in this model of local history. It is based on the belief that each locality can be studied as a social or cultural unit and that patterns of development at the level of town or district are meaningful. Each municipality will obey its own laws of growth, experience its own rhythms of activity and conflict, undergo its own life-cycle of birth and perhaps death. The emphasis, clearly, is upon the common themes in the locality, the themes that all people share despite their age or occupation or religion. The story concerns the community, as if this generalization could encompass everyone at all times, and invites comparisons with the histories of other communities written according to the same plan.

The above chapters, while necessary for an understanding of local society, are far from the complete story of an area. It would be possible to write a history based upon population statistics and settlement strategies and communications routes, we suspect, that would be entirely accurate and yet be almost unrecognizable to the residents of the area. The skeleton of maps and graphs and tables must be made into a living, breathing history with the addition of material on the lives of individuals, the society of the pool hall and bridge club, the conventions of the curling rink, the customs of Hallowe'en, and the contacts with that French community north of town or the Icelanders in the next town east.

Each of the aspects discussed in this second section can reveal something about social life in the community. One must take care, however, to ensure that a history of sports and games, for example, does not become a history solely of the meetings of the rink and fairground committees. The chapters on sources dealing with education, religion, sport, work and families are thus intended to open the way for the study of local cultures, in the plural, and not to suggest that the history of a school or church building should be written in the fashion of a history of the railroad network. Thus, while it may be appropriate to undertake the study of a single local institution, this history should include much more than the succession of formal meetings and motions. Where the Leicester model assumes that one can describe the whole community as a unit, this second approach assumes that "community" itself is a debatable concept. The child emigrant who arrived in Russell as a ward of

Dr. Barnardo's Homes may have little in common with the child of the local doctor or the children of the most affluent farmers in the region. Perhaps they inhabited different "communities," developed different outlooks on life, and had markedly different careers. What are the classes and consciousnesses in each district? How did people find their groups? These questions may not focus on the entire community but may instead take a smaller subject — children's amusements, women's work, courting practices, a harvest excursion, or some other topic limited by time, place, and extent — to secure a sharper picture of a world now past. The great themes of class, ethnicity, and technological change will still be addressed, but they will assume greater meaning because of the wealth of personal detail in which they are clothed. Local history, whether investigated at the level of a parlour conversation or a doctoral dissertation, helps to situate us in time and place. In the classic phrase of the huckster, it can be studied for fun as well as for profit. And, as scholars around the world have suggested, it can provide great intellectual challenges.

CHAPTER 2

The Environment

A SURVEY

The effects of the natural environment upon human society and of humans upon their surroundings are of fundamental importance in a local study. These topics cover a wide area, however, so this chapter will merely raise a few issues for consideration and suggest introductory sources for each.

The present landscape of the province is largely the product of glacial deposits and other alterations made by glaciers during the Ice Age. To begin with, the Pleistocene ice sheets advancing south and west from Hudson Bay acted like bulldozers, planing down the surface and carrying it away. Part of the rock collected was left in mounds, called moraines, which mark the furthest advance of a given ice sheet. Other common types of deposits include drumlins (oval hills of glacial till) and eskers (narrow ridges of sand and gravel). Most of these features run in a north-northwesterly direction parallel to the old glacial fronts. When the glaciers began to retreat, masses of rock and soil trapped in the ice were left on the ground. These materials, an important element in soil formation, are called "glacial till" or "boulder clay." The water from the melting glaciers itself formed huge lakes. Two glacial lakes, Souris, in the southwest, and Agassiz, in the south-central area, have both left large flat basins behind them. Agassiz, the largest glacial lake in North America, covered some 110,000 square miles in its time. When it finally drained bout 6,000 years ago, it exposed the rich valley of the Red. Part of its old basin is now occupied by Lakes Manitoba and Winnipeg. The vast amounts of glacial meltwater feeding these lakes created wide and deep river valleys, such as those now occupied by the Assiniboine and Souris rivers, and left extensive deltas. The area of sand dunes now found between Brandon and Portage la Prairie is the old delta of the Assiniboine where it once met Lake Agassiz, while many other beach ridges and similar formations can be found along the "fossil" shoreline of the lake. The effects of the last glaciation are still an important element of Manitoba's landscape and also of its economic life, for the rich soils of the south are largely developed from various glacial deposits.

A second and related area of environmental study, important especially in farming areas, concerns the nature of soils. These were first classified by the type of soil particle, or texture, in categories which ranged from dune sand and fine sand to sandy loam, clay loam, and stony loam. This has been replaced by a classification system originally devised by Professor J.H. Ellis of the University of Manitoba which takes into account the properties of colour, texture, porosity, and reaction. These determine soil "horizons" and "associations," a classification system which groups soils by parent materials. Soils are also analysed by other interpretative methods, including "agronomic use groups" (soils that behave alike in response to management and treatment for the production of agricultural crops), "soil capability" (categories based on the soil group's potential and limitations for sustained production of common cultivated crops or, in less arable areas, for the production of permanent vegetation), and, finally the "soil productivity index" (a measure to rate the soil's capacity to produce wheat, oats, barley and flax). Further information on these approaches to soil analysis can be found in *Principles and Practices of Commercial Farming*. Soil in a particular district will be described in publications of the Manitoba Soil Survey, Department of Agriculture, Winnipeg. But, first, consult the short-cut prepared by D.M. Loveridge in appendix 2.

In a province where primary products of field and forest are important to the economy, a study of climate is indispensable. Precipitation and temperature patterns remain the fundamental elements of such a study, though the units in which they are described have changed considerably as the science has developed. Both temperature and precipitation fluctuate markedly, of course, but seasonal "probabilities" can be determined and compared to the "normal" or to an average reading. In addition to these basic measurements, scientists are now able to determine with some degree of certainty such phenomena as "potential evapo-transpiration," the amount of water that passes from the ground into the atmosphere when there is no lack of moisture; when this potential is higher than the amount of moisture available from rainfall or irrigation, soil moisture decreases (see Laycock, *Water Deficiency and Surplus Patterns in the Prairie Provinces*). Significantly, using 1921-50 data, Laycock has demonstrated that, on the prairies, evapo-transpiration would use up all the precipitation and much more if it were available; in other words, there are moisture deficits in most areas. The deficit is greatest in southern Saskatchewan (ten inches). In an area extending northwest from Brandon to Dauphin and the Carrot River Valley, an eight-inch moisture deficit occurs only 25 percent of the time, compared with 75 percent in the Medicine Hat region, which demonstrates that the western Manitoba farmer is less likely to be ruined by drought than is the farmer in southern Alberta.

Vegetation distribution has also been studied carefully during the last century, and, when used in conjunction with a number of earlier botanical surveys, these analyses can provide the resources for a kind of "plant history" of a district. The existence within the province of grassland, deciduous and boreal forests, and arctic tundra, and the predominance of forest rather than prairie, are worthy of note. As in the case of soils, so vegetation distribution alters with the passage of time and changes in usage. Fires, for example, have drastically altered the appearance of prairie or forest.

APPROACHES TO ENVIRONMENTAL STUDIES

To the local historian, study of the environment is valuable when it contributes to an understanding of human society. Thus, a profile of certain aspects of the local environment (soils, vegetation, drainage and water resources, normal precipitation patterns), can be of real interest. Significant changes in the state of any of these factors (drought, plant disease, storms and floods, for example) will also be important.

A series of tables or graphs on precipitation patterns and collection of maps with the relevant information on the other topics can create an environmental profile which will clarify the natural history of a district. It is wise to remember that soil quality, vegetation distribution, and drainage systems will change over the years and that a number of estimates taken in different decades will provide a clearer insight into conditions at a given time. The map and survey series mentioned below, especially the township plans, sectional maps, and topographical series, deserve special emphasis because they provide a valuable record of every district taken at intervals (like the census) over an entire century.

SOURCES

Sources for the study of the natural environment in Manitoba are unusually rich. A most reliable and convenient introduction to the range of materials is provided by John Warkentin and Richard I. Ruggles (eds.), *Historical Atlas of Manitoba*: see also T.R. Weir, (ed.) *Economic Atlas of Manitoba*.

Field surveys and topographical maps depict various aspects and most districts of the province in great detail from the 1870s. The "township plans," begun in the 1870s, were the basic surveys for prairie settlement. They included rough estimates of the soil quality, a sketch of vegetation, the presence of marshes and hay meadows, the course of creeks, the position of lakes, trails, and roads, and, where they existed, buildings. The National Map Collection in the Public Archives of Canada (PAC) holds a large number of these surveys and has prepared a free index, organized by section, township and range (Gary Poulin assisted by Francine Cadieux, *Index to Township Plans of the Canadian West*). The field notebooks of the surveyors, though complex, provide remarkable detail on early Manitoba, including buildings as well as size of holdings and, in some cases, areas of crop. Originally housed in the Surveys Branch of the Manitoba Department of Mines, they are now in the Public Archives of Manitoba (PAM).

In 1891, the newly established Topographical Surveys Branch of the federal Department of the Interior began to issue large-scale "sectional maps" of the West to show the ownership of lands, areas yet available for homesteading, and so on. This series underwent many revisions in the following decades, but its maps continued to describe a number of important aspects of the prairie environment, including railroads, trails, post offices, special reserves (Indian lands, timber lands, etc.) and ownership. The PAC National Map Collection holds many of these maps and may be able to direct the researcher to other holdings of relevance to a particular area. By the 1920s the survey was producing genuine topographical maps. Finally, in the late 1920s, the National Topographic System was organized; it created the 1-mile and 4-mile map series using aerial photographs as a base. These scales were revised in the late 1940s, and the present 1:25,000, 1:50,000, 1:250,000, and 1:500,000 map series were created. These may be purchased from the Canada Map Office, Surveys and Mapping Branch, Department of Energy, Mines and Natural Resources, Ottawa. For comments on how to estimate the agricultural potential of a particular district, consult the appendix on the agricultural capability ratings.

CHAPTER 3

Population Studies

A SURVEY

Until the 1860s, European settlement in Manitoba was mainly confined to the Red River Valley where Winnipeg now stands, to the small community of Portage la Prairie on the Assiniboine River, and to a number of fur trade posts. Then in 1867 settlers from Ontario began to move to Manitoba down the newly completed Dawson Road. In general, they settled in a wide circle of communities around Winnipeg, extending from Stony Mountain in the north to Springfield in the east, and from Rivière aux Ilets de Bois in the southwest to Portage la Prairie in the west. By 1870, when Manitoba became a province, the population was only 12,000, almost evenly divided between French and English-speaking groups. However, the 1870s saw the beginning of a large influx of newcomers, many of whom came and settled the land in groups.

The French were the first immigrants to settle as a homogeneous group. They came in the mid-1870s and, as the Metis moved west to the Saskatchewan Valley or Montana, they took up the vacated lands south of Winnipeg near such settlements as Ste. Anne-des-Chênes, Ile-des-Chênes, Letellier, and St-Malo. They were soon followed by the Mennonites, who had been granted two large tracts of land by the Dominion government: the East Reserve southeast of Winnipeg around Steinbach, and the West Reserve on the west side of the Red River near Winkler and Gretna. A third group migration took place after the volcanic eruption of Iceland's Mount Hecla, when a large party of Icelanders settled on the west shore of Lake Winnipeg in 1875. Despite considerable hardship, they persevered in their Republic of New Iceland and, after the 1881 extension of Manitoba's boundaries, eventually were brought under the authority of the provincial government.

---

* The complex story of the movements of the Native peoples of the province is discussed in detail in chapter 13.

During the late 1870s, settlement truly fanned out across the prairies. A long string of communities extended from Emerson on the Red westward to Deloraine along the Boundary Commission Trail, which served as the main transportation route out of Emerson after 1872-3. Another string of settlements grew up along the Carlton trail (from Portage to Edmonton) including Westbourne, Gladstone, and Shoal Lake. When railways crossed the plains, they replaced trails as the magnet for town development, beginning with the Pembina Branch (from St. Boniface to the American border, 1878) which perpetuated the use of the St. Paul to Winnipeg cart trail of the 1850s and 1860s, and the Canadian Pacific, whose tracks spanned the province from the eastern boundary to Brandon by September 1881. Branch-line construction in the next two decades either followed or directed settlement, depending on the circumstances in each district, but in every case it determined the fate of aspiring towns.

One of the most important contributions to Manitoba's population was the immigration boom between 1895 and 1913, when thousands of Canadians, Britons, and Europeans settled vast tracts of land in the districts farthest from Winnipeg, including the Dauphin area and the Swan River Valley.

The First World War temporarily halted immigration to Manitoba. Hostility to German and central European immigrants and the economic depression which followed the conflict extended this pause into the early 1920s, but by 1924 the depression had subsided and immigration resumed at a moderate pace. It would never regain the momentum it had enjoyed before the war, however, because most of the arable land was taken.

The population of rural Manitoba reached its peak in 1931. The growth of small towns continued at a slower pace, however, even through the Depression. Town population then decreased in all but a few centres and, after 1951, the number of people leaving the farm for larger urban centres increased markedly. Some towns managed to maintain their numbers in the next two decades, but, unless their leaders have attracted new services and industries, they may be doomed to a slow decline in size and vitality.

APPROACHES TO POPULATION STUDIES

What can we learn from population records? The most significant product will be tables and graphs which sketch an outline of the community for a hundred years or more. The total population, its composition by age group, by national origin and religion, by size of family, all will change. The nature of the household (number of lodgers and other residents), will change, too, and so will the composition of the labour force and the type of farm enterprise. What are these changes and how can they be explained? Here are questions enough to provide a solid introduction to the history of a district.

SOURCES

Manitoba is more fortunate than the other prairie provinces with regard to censuses. The Provincial Archives of Manitoba and the Hudson's Bay Company Archives contain Red River Settlement censuses that began as early as 1814 and continued at irregular intervals until 1868. All contain lists of the population at Red River and most add considerable information on such items as livestock, implements, cultivated acreage, and buildings.

The next major census of Manitoba was taken on the province's entry into Confederation in 1870. One copy, nearly complete, is available in the PAM and another can be found in the Sessional Papers of Canada (V:20, 1871, p. 91). It simply lists the residents of the new province by household and by age and occupation. Additional information about this census can be found in the Alexander Morris papers and the Louis Riel papers, both located in the Provincial Archives. Manitoba was first included in the complete Dominion census of 1881.

While the censuses contain general statistics on Manitoba, there exist several good studies of a more specific nature. These include an excellent work by C.B. Davidson, *The Population of Manitoba*, which covers the period 1881-1936. For population and socio-economic statistics for the period 1951-71 unquestionably the best source is a Manitoba Department of Industry study with accompanying maps entitled *Regional Analysis Program: Southern Manitoba*. Unfortunately this study does not cover the entire province, but it does include the majority of small towns. An introduction to quantitative records is provided in M.C. Urquhart and K.A.H. Buckley (eds.), *Historical Statistics of Canada*.

A history of the decennial census was published in the 1931 edition and a revision of the general population totals, 1871-1951, according to modern boundary definitions, accompanied the 1951 census.

These census records can provide an introduction to almost every aspect of the economy and society in a local district. They should be regarded as one starting point for any local study and, therefore, should be photocopied and stored in a local library for use by students. A complete collection of these tables for a single community would amount to several hundred pages, would accordingly cost about twenty to thirty dollars, and the compilation would require several days' work.

The Dominion census provides, first, the number of residents in a district and incorporated town, depending on the decade, and gives details of age, marital status, and sex. In other tables, it describes the nature of their housing, the number of members of each religion, the racial or national origin of the residents and their birthplace, the size of their farms and the number of acres of crop (sometimes with estimates of production for each type of crop), pasture, garden, and woodland. In some years, the census separates the owners and renters of land, lists the number and type of farm animals, the production of wool, cheese, and butter, the products of the fur trade, fishing, and forestry, and the amount of shipping. In others, it considers the number of retail stores and the volume of their sales. In recent years, it has provided a careful study of the labour force by occupation and by earnings and an equally detailed survey of farm equipment. Often, these records are sufficiently detailed to permit study for some purposes (especially total population of individual townships as well as towns and municipalities), but for other purposes, the census districts encompass entire federal constituencies with separate entries only for the urban centres and municipalities.

The provincial or prairie census, called the quinquennial census, varies in detail but is equally valuable. Thus, an important statistical summary of the provincial society has been issued by the federal government for every tenth year since 1881, and comparable statements have been prepared for the half-decade in every tenth year from 1886 to the present (except 1896). It is best to assume that one constant unit of information for your area will be the municipality, and that it will constitute one focus of a study. Most towns which are now over 1000 in population will probably be covered consistently in the tables, but there is no guarantee that smaller settlements can be followed so easily.

Further information on small towns and rural municipalities is contained in a series of municipal censuses. These are available for the years 1896, 1904, 1906, 1907, 1909, 1910, 1913 and 1914, and are found in the Municipal Commissioners Report of the following year in the Manitoba Sessional Papers. Thus the 1896 census is found in the Sessional Papers of 1897. These censuses contain data on population, agriculture, taxation and assessment values.

Information on vital statistics at the local level is difficult to obtain, but some data can be found in the Annual Reports of the Manitoba Department of Agriculture and Immigration for the years 1889, 1890, 1894, and 1898 to 1912. As with the municipal censuses, these reports are found in the volume of the following year. Data is provided on the number of births, deaths and marriages.

A final warning concerns the area covered by a census division. Town and municipal boundaries change, producing marked changes in the census tables. Maps of these changing boundaries must be obtained before the census can be of value (consult the Historic Resources Branch, Manitoba Department of Cultural Affairs and Historical Resources).

One of the most distressing problems encountered by students of Manitoba local history is the lack of statistical information pertaining to unincorporated communities, which form the bulk of communities with fewer than 3000 residents. The Manitoba Bureau of Statistics does possess an unofficial listing of these communities for the years 1941, 1951, and 1961; though its accuracy remains in doubt, this list is apparently the only available source on such settlements.

When trying to locate information about the population of a particular community, the Manitoba Directory, 1876-9, and the city directories of later years are invaluable. These volumes provide the names of many professional and businessmen of the province, by community, as well as a list of all the eligible voters in the community. Similar in content is *Henderson's Manitoba and North West Territories Gazeteer and Directory*. A list of these directories is contained in appendix 4. The volumes for 1881 through 1908 are available in the Legislative Library. In addition to these sources, some municipalities periodically undertook municipal censuses. A quick check with the appropriate municipal records office will reveal if such records exist for the community or district being studied.

While these statistical tables can aid greatly in the reconstruction of an area's past life, their limitations must be realized. To begin with, the census, like all human undertakings, is subject to human error. For that reason it is well to check, if possible, several sources that contain the same sort of statistics, and, by comparing them, ascertain the most likely figure. Another problem with the census is changing definitions, several of which have affected the Manitoba records. In 1881 and in 1912 the boundaries of the province were considerably extended, and the population rose accordingly. While no account of the 1881 change seems to have been taken, in 1912 the statistics for the 1911 census were changed to include the 1912 increases. This change was subsequently acknowledged in all other censuses. The other main problem of definition concerns the terms "urban" and "rural". Up to and including the 1941 Dominion census, urban simply meant all those cities, towns and villages which were incorporated, while rural included everyone else. In 1951 the definition of urban was altered to include all communities with over 1000 people. Rural took in everyone remaining. The final change of this type came in 1956 when urban was expanded to include the unincorporated fringe of major centres, such as Winnipeg.

CHAPTER 4

Transportation and Communications

A SURVEY

The lack of an efficient communications and transportation network held back the Red River economy during the first half of the nineteenth century. With the establishment of such a network in the succeeding half-century the conditions for Manitoba's rapid development were in place. The revolution in technology which has taken place in the first half of the twentieth century has created even greater changes in this province, to the point that we may now question whether "local neighbourhoods" even exist in the days of instant international communications.

Prior to the European occupation of Manitoba, the chief modes of transportation used in the area were the canoe and the dogsled. When horses arrived on the prairies in the eighteenth century, they were used for both passenger and freight traffic. The introduction of the horse and travois so transformed the speed and range of travel that well-worn trails soon criss-crossed the prairies.

Manitoba's water routes were the avenues of the fur trade from the mid-seventeenth century, when Hudson's Bay Company men came from the north and the voyageurs of New France, and later the North-West Company, came from the east. Between them they employed a system of waterways which extended across the Rocky Mountains in the west and to the Mississippi River and the Gulf of Mexico in the south. As they moved further inland, a series of trading posts was established along the river routes, supplied by canoes and York boats from the larger trade centres on Hudson Bay and Lake Superior.

When the fur trade expanded in the 1770s and plains provisions became the staple food of the canoe brigades, an efficient means of land transportation became essential. Such a means was found in the Red River cart, drawn by horses or oxen, which came into widespread use after 1800. Because it combined ease of construction and repair with capaciousness and versatility, it was ideal for transporting goods and people across the barren prairies. By the mid-nineteenth century, the Red River cart was Manitoba's principal means of transport, and it remained so for another quarter-century.

The role of the cart brigade was first reduced in the 1860s by the American Civil War and the threat of Sioux attack, and later, in 1867, by the introduction of the springless buckboard. Also competing for the passenger trade was the stagecoach, which first ran from Fort Abercrombie to Fort Garry in September 1871. More serious competition for the cart developed when the Hudson's Bay Company, dissatisfied with its seasonally ice-bound northern route, turned to the use of steamboats. After the first steamboat, the *Anson Northup*, reached Fort Garry from Fort Abercrombie in 1859, the H.B.C. began shipping half its annual trade from Fort Garry to St. Paul, Minnesota. From there it went either to New York or to Montreal and then on to Europe. The volume of this trade accelerated boat-building and soon many vessels plied the Red River. This river trade expanded within a decade to take in both the Assiniboine River and Lake Winnipeg. Yet, for all their efficiency, the water routes were useful only in summer and, even then, only as long as water levels remained high. When levels dropped, as they did during the 1860s, the cart brigades regained much of the trade.

When both carts and steamboats were in service, the cart brigade became an extension of river transportation. This complementary system opened wide a new entrance to the Northwest. Settlers slowly began to come to Manitoba via a rail and steamboat route through St. Paul and Pembina. At the border, they loaded their possessions onto carts and proceeded westward down the Boundary Commission Trail in search of a homestead or headed north to the growing town of Winnipeg.

Manitoba's postal service was greatly improved by the evolution of new transportation routes. Originally, all mail was carried by the Hudson's Bay Company's twice-yearly service, but a virtual revolution in mail service occurred in 1853 when a once-a-month service was started between Fort Garry and Fort Ripley, Minnesota. This service expanded with time, and all forms of transport — carts, stagecoaches and steamers — were used to improve it. During the 1870s still more expansion took place and regular service was provided for Manitoba communities. In areas where there was no regular postal service, members of the North-West Mounted Police often carried the mails. Thus, the growth of the postal service in Manitoba reflected the general improvement in communications systems.

In many parts of the world, the telegraph accompanied the railroad into new territories, but this boon to rapid long-distance communication first reached Winnipeg in 1871 as an extension of an American telegraph system.

Later, telegraph lines were constructed along the Canadian Pacific rail line and subsequently along other railways. Manitoba's communications web now consisted not only of trails and rivers but of wires as well.

The railway, however, was the innovation which forever ended the remoteness not only of Manitoba but of the entire northwest. The Pembina Branch Railway, the Canadian Pacific Railway, and the branches which followed provided access to far-away markets and also brought regular news from the outside and shipments of the world's produce to village stores.

While rural Manitoba was becoming accustomed to the telegraph, Winnipeg began experimenting with the newly invented telephone. The first telephone was installed in 1878; four years later the city could boast ten. Gradually the telephone spread outside Winnipeg, with the centres of Brandon, Selkirk, and Portage la Prairie receiving service first. In the early 1900s, long-distance service was initiated, and in 1908 the Roblin government took control of the entire network, most of which was privately owned, through the Manitoba Telephone System. Forty years later the province had over a million miles of telephone lines and it was possible to call anywhere in the world.

Daily newspapers accompanied the telegraph into the province and soon became a prominent part of urban life. Every town that could afford a weekly hastened to establish one or even two in the expectation that the paper would repay the investment many times over. These journals are, needless to say, of immense value to the local historian. Several aspects of newspaper history might be noted here. First, many weeklies used a "packaged features" section from an early date. Produced in Winnipeg or further afield, these collections of fiction, household hints, and children's games were the forerunners of the modern weekend colour supplements and should not be mistaken for the local editor's own product. Second, from late in the nineteenth century, the larger dailies would often establish links with a telegraph news service which would "collect" and edit stories from across the country and around the world. Like the features supplements, the content of these wire service stories was not determined by the local editors. For information on newspapers that have been published in the province, see D.M. Loveridge, *Historical Directory of Manitoba Newspapers, 1859-1978.* For the history of rural newspapers in Manitoba, consult "A Survey of the History of Rural Journalism in Manitoba 1875-1976" (Historic Resources Branch, Government of Manitoba, 1976) by the same author, available in the Legislative Library.

Similar progress occurred in the road system. In 1870 Manitoba had some 700 miles of road, chiefly rough trails, the responsibility for which resided entirely with the provincial government. Ten years later all roads were placed under the jurisdiction of municipal governments, a move which often increased the taxes levied within municipalities. In 1912 a cost-sharing arrangement was worked out between the province and the municipalities in order to meet the growing demand for good roads. This demand was stimulated by mass production of the automobile. In 1910 only 1715 vehicles were registered in the province; by 1930 that figure had jumped to 78,850 and the Manitoba government had begun to experiment with hard surface roads. From this constant effort to improve the existing road system has come our modern system of interchanges, trunk highways, and secondary roads. Highway construction has been significant for rural communities. Because the private car makes it easy to travel great distances, our social attitudes have changed. In addition, the possibility of comfortable trips to towns thirty or fifty or even a hundred miles away influences trade patterns and often spells the end of the smallest communities which cannot offer a large variety of services. On the other hand, better roads have assured some communities more rapid access to distant markets, better service to consumers, and more tourist trade, all of which make such centres grow.

Extending the reach of Manitobans even further was the growth of aviation after the First World War. At first planes were used mainly to open up the north, but the development of Western Canada Airways in 1926 and the Prairie Air Mail in 1930 made the aviation industry an indispensable component of the western transportation system. With the establishment of Trans Canada Airlines (Air Canada) in 1937 and of Canadian Pacific Air Lines, Manitoba was more than ever in touch with the world.

The beginning of radio broadcasting in the 1920s and television in the 1950s made instant communication with the world possible. In one century Manitoba went from isolation to cosmopolitanism on the grandest scale. Every citizen has been profoundly influenced by this revolution in the technology of transportation and communications.

APPROACHES TO TRANSPORTATION STUDIES

Transportation and communications networks constitute one of the basic elements upon which society is built. The first task of the student, therefore, is to determine how a local community's transport network evolved. How is it related to provincial and local topography? Was it on a fur trade route or cart trail? Did it have steamboat service and, if so, what were the consequences for economic development and the growth of population? When and in what circumstances did regular mail and telegraph services begin? Did a newspaper begin shortly thereafter? Was your area developed after a railway arrived or did settlement precede rail construction? Which railway company built the line in your area? Was there a debate over the rail route, were concessions granted by the local council to the company, were local directors involved in the company, or did company directors speculate in the development of your town site? Has your station or line been a subject of debate during the recent talk of rail line abandonment; if so, why? When did the telephone arrive in your area? Did a local or private company precede the government-owned system? What part have the road system or airplanes played in the history of your area? When did radio and television arrive and when did your area become a part of the national and international networks? Finally, and in sum, how have the changes in communications technology during the last century affected the course of your community's history?

SOURCES

A wealth of information exists on communications and transportation in Manitoba. As usual, the census is a good starting place. The censuses taken by the Hudson's Bay Company in the nineteenth century give the number and type of water-craft and carts owned by the Red River settlers, as well as the number of draught animals per settler. These are located in the Hudson's Bay Company Archives.

Nineteenth-century censuses of Canada are useful in so far as they provide general information on water-craft, their numbers, tonnage, and average size. Unfortunately the census division is the smallest unit for which statistics are given. Other federal government sources that provide helpful general information include annual reports on shipping and navigation, on railways and canals, and on the postal service. These can be found by consulting the Sessional Papers of Canada (see the annual index therein).

Of great importance to anyone seeking information on transportation is the Transportation Collection in the Public Archives of Manitoba. Its John E. Parker Collection, for example, includes correspondence, data, and photographs on steamboats circa 1858-1946. The Transportation Collection also contains a 1910 list of automobile owners and chauffeurs of Manitoba (complete with addresses), the scrapbooks of the Manitoba Motor League, 1915-22, CPR Timetables, 1881-93, Port of Winnipeg Shipping Registers, 1875-97, and other material on almost every mode of transportation in Manitoba.

Another type of introduction to transportation topics is provided by the *Historical Atlas of Manitoba*, edited by J.H. Warkentin and R.I. Ruggles.

The Historic Files of the Manitoba Department of Transportation, 1870-1962, contain useful materials on the development of the province's road system, as well as detailed descriptions of many trails, 1870-1900. This is the source to check in order to ascertain which trail your community was located on, and that trail's exact location. These files are housed in the Provincial Archives.

   Henderson's Directory, located in the Provincial Library, is another valuable source of information on transportation for local historians. Beginning in 1881, the directory gives a detailed breakdown of livery stables, express offices, stage companies, telegraph offices, steamboat companies and their owners and operators in each community. With this information, you can reconstruct the history of transportation and communication for any community in the province from 1878 to 1908.

   Information on post offices can most easily be obtained through the use of the *Canadian Almanac* (1842-present). This storehouse of information gives the name of every post office, its location according to township and electoral district, and its postmaster. Through this source it is possible to discover much of a community's postal history. The Postmaster-General's Annual Reports, in Canada Sessional Papers, are also valuable, for they provide the annual receipts and number and value of money orders for each post office. These figures can be used to determine the trading orbits of local communities. The best example of this technique is contained in John Warkentin's "Western Canada in 1886," (see bibliography under "Postal Service").

   Telephone records, which have been kept by Manitoba Government Telephones (now MTS) since it began in 1908, are still extant. Information about when your community received its first telephone service, about changes in its type of service, and especially about early operators and linemen can best be obtained by contacting the Winnipeg office of the Manitoba Telephone System.

   Information on radio and television is at once easier and more difficult to accumulate. A free publication of the Public Archives of Canada, National Map Collection, entitled *Telecommunications: The Canadian Experience / Télécommunications: L'Expérience canadienne*, edited by James W. Knight, presents not only maps of road and telegraph systems but also of telephones, radio broadcasting and television. In the latter cases, Mr. Knight demonstrates that PAC maps can be used for the study of reception areas of radio transmission from the 1920s to the present and of television from the 1950s to the present.

   Individual radio and television stations also maintain records, though they should be approached in advance to determine whether their files are of use and available for study. The Richardson Archives, Richardson Building, Winnipeg, has at times permitted serious research into the records of such family holdings as radio stations and airlines. Some of the records of the French-language radio station, CKSB, are deposited with the archives of La Société Historique de Saint-Boniface.

One problem with the study of radio and television is that their programmes are rarely produced locally. In the modern era, the study of communications becomes a study of multinational rather than local culture. But local variations do, of course, remain, and they can be studied for their own sake.

CHAPTER 5

Agriculture

A SURVEY

Agriculture was the economic foundation of modern Manitoba. The native people had experience in cultivating plants, but their lifestyle was semi-nomadic and their agriculture impermanent. Fur traders too tried their skill at tilling the soil, but their garden plots gave only a few crops for immediate consumption. The Red River settlers struggled along with subsistence farming, but their husbandry was not well adapted to the land and climate and their transportation system would not sustain large-scale exports. Developments in agricultural science, farm technology, and railways led to a new era of agricultural production.

The Canadian government established an effective administration to control and guide agricultural settlement after the transfer of Manitoba in 1870 (see appendix 1). With the first export of prairie wheat in 1876, grain merchandising companies were formed in Winnipeg, and plans for grain purchase and storage were devised. It is said that the first western elevator was constructed at Niverville in 1879, but the flat warehouse was more common in these early years. As the annual grain surplus grew, the export of wheat underwrote the formation of private elevator companies. Six elevators had been constructed by 1882, ninety by 1890, in addition to over a hundred flat warehouses. The total storage capacity in 1890 was four million bushels.

The flour milling business kept pace with the growth in wheat production. In the early 1880s, the new Hungarian steel roller milling process reached Winnipeg and, by a happy coincidence, proved especially suitable for the production of white flour from western hard spring wheat. Many towns soon had their own mill which served the farmers and residents of the district.

In its early stages, the handling of western grain was haphazard, with many independent grain firms following different buying and selling policies. In an effort to make the grain business more uniform, the Winnipeg Board of

Trade established a Grain Exchange in 1883. Though this enterprise was soon dissolved, it provided the experience which led to the formation of the Grain and Produce Exchange four years later, the first large step in a series of attempts to bring uniformity to grain purchasing and marketing. The problem of consistent grading principles, another important issue, was also addressed at this time. After many protests by farmers, the federal government began to intervene more vigorously in the trade in 1898. Royal commissions and acts of Parliament in the next two decades provided the framework for the Canadian grain trade which has lasted to this day.

This federal intervention, like the provincial involvement in the same era, took place because of the pressures exerted by farmers. As the goals of the farmers became more urgent and precise, they organized into associations which could exert more influence upon public policy. These farmers argued that an unjust and inadequate line elevator system, discriminatory rail freight rates, and an unfair terminal elevator system could be reformed only by common action. Farm organizations were not new in Manitoba, having emerged in the 1870s (the Grange), the mid-1880s (the Manitoba and North-West Farmers' Protective Union, an offshoot of provincial rights agitation), and the early 1890s (the Patrons of Industry, descendant of American and Ontario protest). But the new Manitoba Grain Growers' Association (MGGA), founded in 1903 (renamed the United Farmers of Manitoba in 1920), was a more powerful and effective spokesman for farm interests. First fruit of its activities was a campaign to reform grain-marketing practices which resulted in the creation of the Grain Growers' Grain Company (GGG) in 1906 (a selling agency) and, in 1910, an agreement with Premier Roblin to establish a government-owned elevator company. A dismal failure, the company was dissolved in 1912 and most of its elevators ended up in the GGG Company, re-named the United Grain Growers in 1917. The MGGA also participated in the founding of the Canadian Council of Agriculture in 1909, and of the great organ of farm organization in that era, the *Grain Growers' Guide*. With the end of federal involvement in international grain marketing (1917 to 1920), Manitoba farmers were active in the drive to create a new voluntary selling agency, the Pool, in 1923-4. In the same period, farmers took their dissatisfaction into the political system helping to elect a Progressive government in the province in 1922 and returning several Progressive members in the federal election of 1921 (see chapter 7 on politics for these and later developments).

Farm organization continued and expanded in the following decades. Specialization of farm production has resulted in the creation of associations for dairy and stock growers, vegetable producers, and many others, on the one hand, and political differences have resulted in the rise of such different groups as the Palliser Wheat Growers, the National Farmers' Union, and the Manitoba Farm Bureau.

Another theme in agricultural history is the local adoption of scientific and technological advances. Reapers, threshing machines, combines, trucks, and rubber-wheeled tractors arrived at different times in different districts and achieved general acceptance at varying speeds. The factors influencing the purchase of new equipment, whether economic or social, can be assessed, but if generalizations are to be made about the relative rate of adaptation of say, Mennonites and Ukrainians, to new farming methods, they must be sustained by systematic investigation. The same questions may be addressed to new developments in plant breeding, types of crop, and innovations in cultivation techniques, or the use of herbicides.

Agricultural education, sponsored by local agricultural representatives of the provincial government and by the University of Manitoba Faculty of Agriculture, has also played a role in the life of many communities (see the bibliography for references).

APPROACHES TO AGRICULTURAL STUDIES

It is helpful to construct a set of tables and graphs showing the agricultural economy of a crop district or rural municipality. This outline should include reports on cultivated acreage for each crop, yield (where possible), prices (if necessary using the annual averages), and comparable data for animals and dairy products. Such tables will permit investigation not only of the farm economy but of related social matters such as population changes and the state of nearby towns.

Graphs can also be created to illustrate the number and size of farms in the municipality, as well as the number of agricultural labourers, amount of capital invested, and type of farm machinery on each farm. These visual aids can clarify the history of a district by emphasizing important turning points and providing the structure around which a narrative can be built.

There are many other useful approaches. What is the history of farm organization in the district? Are there papers related to farm groups in someone's possession? What is the story of elevator service in the town? Has there been a mill in your district? Did local people make presentations to the Royal Commissions on Grain? Is the farm economy discussed in the local newspaper? What was the local experience during the drought years of the 1930s or in the years of rural depopulation after the Second World War? When did the combine come into general use? The swather? The truck? Was a

Farmers' Institute or agricultural society active in the district?

A study of the local fair can provide interesting insights into agricultural history because this annual event is so often a showcase for farm products and new farming techniques as well as an occasion for newspapers to reflect upon past achievements and present needs.

SOURCES

The earliest sources of statistical information about Manitoba agriculture are the censuses of the Red River settlement mentioned in the chapter on population. The Hudson's Bay Company censuses are especially helpful because they report on the population, acreage, livestock, and crops of each Red River farm.

Statistics for the post-1870 period begin in the Manitoba census of 1885-6. Figures are given by electoral districts (5) and sub-districts (106), for such things as animals and animal products, field products (types, yields, acreages), land quantities, number of farm operators, and so on. Comparative tables supply figures for 1881 and 1886. These agricultural statistics are continued in subsequent censuses.

Still in a general vein, the Dominion Bureau of Statistics (now Statistics Canada) has issued a series of useful handbooks: *Field Crops, 1908-62; Farm Income, 1926-65; Trends in Canadian Agriculture.* In each case, the information is organized by province. The booklet dealing with farm income also contains an excellent overview of factors affecting net farm income since 1926.

For more specific information on local areas, the Manitoba Department of Agriculture issues the following continuous publications: Annual Report of the Minister (or Department) of Agriculture and Immigration 1880- ; Manitoba Crop Bulletins, 1883- ; and Manitoba Yearbook of Agriculture 1963- (which contains information for the period since 1926). These sources can be supplemented by a wheat map of Manitoba, 1897, which gives the quantities of grain produced by each Manitoba community for that year. This is found on the front page of the Winnipeg *Tribune*, 18 December 1897.

Commissions of investigation into agriculture, royal or not, have produced much of interest to the student of history. Grain enquiries have been conducted by the federal government in 1899, 1906, 1925, 1931, and 1938. A Manitoba commission on farm organizations completed its report in 1962. A two-volume *Agriculture Survey*, sponsored by the provincial government, completed in 1921, is unusually rich in information on Manitoba.

The major farm organizations, like the Manitoba Pool Elevators, also issue annual reports.

For primary information about the important post-1900 period of agrarian cooperation, consult the farmers' periodicals, *The Grain Growers Guide, The Nor'West Farmer, and The Farmers' Advocate,* all of which can be found in the Provincial Library. If futher information is required, the latest edition of Statistics Canada's *Catalogue* may supply some references.

The staff of the Rural Archives in the Community Resource Centre, Brandon University, is especially interested in agricultural history and should be consulted to determine whether this collection can be of use in your project. The papers of the Manitoba Pool are located in the Rural Archives.

CHAPTER 6

Business

A SURVEY

The production and exchange of goods and services is the lifeblood of a community. Merchants, native and European, provided the focus for early settlements on the prairies, and their successors continued to be leaders of local society after the creation of Manitoba. Industries based on local demands and resources — carpentry and woodworking, grist mills and distilling — also preceded Dominion control of the West, while others, such as brick and clay works, glassmaking, and quarries developed later. Local means of finance often developed with the growth of a small town, giving way to larger institutions around the turn of the twentieth century. These activities — commerce, industry, finance — were a source of vitality for many years. That some have since disappeared and others have changed dramatically should make the telling of their stories doubly significant.

The pattern of growth in small-town businesses was probably repeated many times on the Canadian and American frontiers. A combination of trading post, stopping place, general store, and post office would be established along a transportation route or, in the case of towns where the railroad arrive first, a station and a stopping place would be constructed almost simultaneously. Wherever economically viable, that is, about five to ten miles apart on every rail line, hamlets would grow into villages and perhaps towns. A few new businesses would be established and, if a market could be found, the list of enterprises would become increasingly diversified. Hotels, restaurants, livery stables, blacksmith shops, hardware stores, real estate and insurance agents, implement dealers, dress and millinery shops, bakers, butchers, newspapers, and grocery stores would constitute the business community in these growing towns. A businessmen's organization might be created to seek still other services — to woo a doctor and build a hospital, to finish the sidewalk system, to build a community hall or skating rink. From the 1880s to about 1914, these towns knew the uncertainty of the boom and bust cycle, but their business leaders were probably sustained by the exhilaration of certain progress and the challenge of constant change.

Though their history remains unwritten, these business leaders must have confronted drastic changes during the next three decades. The growth of most little towns was slowed by the First World War. Postwar economic uncertainty hurt rural and urban Manitoba alike. The decade of depression in the thirties, though not as severe as in Saskatchewan, offered no easy road to prosperity. Thus, the spread of the automobile, the radio, and telephone, and the emergence of a society based on mass production, mass advertising, and mass consumption, coupled with the instability of the agricultural economy, confined rural service centres to the roles they had played in 1914. By the end of the Second World War, the commercial leaders of many towns must have found their ranks depleted and their functions disappearing. For every community that survived and grew stronger in the next three decades — and thirty or forty probably have done so — another four will have declined in population.

Whether stable, growing, or disappearing, the small town relied on its merchants to provide leadership. Continuity in the mercantile group over a long period of years and the passing of family businesses from one generation to the next may be a principal reason for the survival of some service centres. On the other hand, a drastic change in the business leadership — a transition from one ethnic group to another, for example — might also signal a revival of a town's fortunes.

A number of related themes may be represented in the history of rural merchants. One is the growth of the co-operative movement in western Canada in the first four decades of the twentieth century. Originally associated with grain marketing and later with bulk-buying schemes, the growth of local co-operative stores had an impact upon the business community in many towns. Secondly, the growth of the mail-order catalogue in the early twentieth century undercut some local merchants. Third, the national chain-store movement arrived on the prairies in the 1920s, sweeping hardware, grocery, and meat-packing stores into bigger units with standardized advertising and management techniques. (Whether this affected the local community is a moot point, however, for Smith's General Store might well become the local outlet of a supermarket chain without changing much more than the sign outside and some of the brand names on the shelves. Thus, one must determine whether the local store owner simply purchased a franchise or became an employee of the national firm before one begins to comment on the retail changes.) And, finally, the spread of the mass communications techniques mentioned above introduced Manitobans to the virtues of national or multinational "brand-name" goods and uniform production of everything from soup and crackers to work gloves and dining-room chairs.

Decisions on site have always been important to urban communities. The transportation and grain industries merit special attention in this regard. Naturally, the choice of one town as a sectional or divisional point on the rail line has an effect not only on the size of the population but on every other aspect of community life; conversely, closure of a rail station or the end of passenger service can be a severe blow. Decisions to concentrate grain-handling facilities in one town or to remove them from another can be equally significant in the history of an entire district. Other local services, such as the consolidated school, the hospital, the bank, and the old folks' home, can also shape the direction of a community. In recent years, government and business decisions on the location of services have become as critical to the fate of towns as they were in 1880s.

The story of local industries is often similar to the history of the retail merchant group. Associated with local resources — grain, timber, clay, sand, dairy herds, minerals, fish — these industries might have developed in the first generation of the prairie boom. Many of them, particularly those producing construction materials and flour, did not survive the economic crises and the pressures for concentration of ownership after 1913. Very few survived the Depression to continue into the postwar era. Interestingly, a number have been established in the last two decades, suggesting that the trend to centralization of production in this province may be slowing down.

Banking and credit facilities are significant in every community and doubly so in areas that depend on the erratic payments from grain production. The earliest finance facilities in the province were often provided by merchants who, in their turn, operated on credit granted by wholesalers and manufacturers or by metropolitan banks. A second early source of financial assistance was the private banker, a citizen with sufficient capital to embark upon mortgage and other lending ventures. His services were necessary in early Manitoba because a small town could not attract branches of chartered banks before the district was well established. Most private banks in Manitoba, like those of Alloway and Champion, or Allan Brydges and Company, had their head offices in Winnipeg and branches in a number of small towns. Nine private banks existed in 1885 and nineteen in 1895.

It was common for chartered banks (those regulated by the federal government) to move into a new community by taking over a private bank while retaining the former banker as manager. Chartered banks and their branches grew rapidly during the economic boom years of 1881-2. When the boom collapsed, however, inflation was so widespread that many citizens became insolvent. The subsequent branch failures reduced the numbers of branches in Manitoba and not until 1900 did mergers again become regular occurrences. By 1914, the banking system as we know it, with a few large chartered banks and many branch offices, was solidly established. The last "Western" bank prior to the 1970s, the Union Bank of Canada, failed in 1925 and was absorbed into the Royal Bank system.

Another important financial institution in rural districts was the credit union, which became an important factor in rural Manitoba during the 1930s. Because credit unions were local operations, they could have considerable influence on the development of a town, and, therefore, should be considered as worthy of special study.

APPROACHES TO LOCAL BUSINESS HISTORY

The first step in studying local business history is to determine which businesses existed, when they were founded, and what was the course of their development. It is possible to learn their approximate annual sales and capitalization, for example, and to determine when mergers or changes in ownership took place.

Once this essential descriptive work is completed, the study can proceed along a number of lines. Students might ask why certain businesses and industries developed or disappeared. They might investigate the owners and managers as a group to determine whether generalizations can be made about their origins, outlook, or political influence. They might investigate broader trends in the economy, considering whether the fate of local businesses is determined by the fortune of the district or by trends in the national and international economy. The mail order house, for example, and the cooperative buying or selling agency, were often at the centre of local debates concerning town business fortunes and town-farm relations.

Local industries may have been owned and operated by one family or by a few investors, and have had only a small number of employees, but they were often important in the economy and in the politics of town and district. A study of them can provide an insight into the larger forces at work in the nation (centralization of production in metropolitan centres, for example), and into the social structure of the town. One may be able to establish a picture of the owners and managers by income, by ethnic groups, by house type, and by social and political standing. How does this picture compare with that of the work force? Were there ever disagreements over salaries or working conditions and, if so, how were they settled? Can one conclude that small towns are classless societies? Since the history of small businesses on the prairies has yet to be written, these remain only suggestions rather than rules for interpretation.

SOURCES

A history of local business must begin with a study of directories and atlases to determine the nature and number of local mercantile and industrial operations. This can best be established by the use of the provincial directories (see appendix 4), fire insurance atlases (PAM), the *Reference Books of Dun and Bradstreet of Canada Limited* (located in their Toronto office and available for consultation if prior permission is obtained), and the *Manitoba Trade Directory* (annual 1949-   , available at the Provincial Library). The *Canadian Almanac* (annual, 1842-   , University of Manitoba, Dafoe Library) lists banks, branches and managers and, after 1924, membership on Boards of Trade and Chambers of Commerce.

More extensive information will be found in the Dominion census statistics on retail trade (available for censuses after 1931; see chapter 3) and on industries (available since the 1881 census), and in three Manitoba government publications: the Department of Industry and Commerce, *Town Trading Surveys* (1964-66), its *Community Reports* (1968-   , annual) and the Carvalho-Page study entitled *Regional Analysis Program: Southern Manitoba 1951-1971*, published by the Manitoba Department of Industry and Commerce in 1972. Also worthy of notice are the *Byers Western Industrial Directories* (1928-   , annual), *Manitoba Industrial Topics* (monthly 1941-1950), and the April issue of *Towns and Cities* (1954-   , quarterly) which is devoted to the prairies. For districts with substantial industries, the *Labour Gazette* (1900-   , monthly) and the *Annual Report* of the Department of Labour (1900-   , annual) will provide greater information on the work force, though principally in industries where unions have been established.

Local council and tax records and building permits will provide some indication of the state of individual companies. The Manitoba Department of Corporate Affairs and Environment, Corporations Branch, 10th Flr, 405 Broadway Ave., Winnipeg, R3C 3L6 contains records for many (but not all) provincial companies, including information on ownership, purpose, capitalization, and some annual reports.

Companies with federal charters were required to file a brief report listing directors, share capital, and intent, which was printed in the Sessional Papers under the annual report of the Secretary of State. Records of companies with operations in a particular area may be lodged in the Public

Archives of Manitoba or another archival collection, so a quick check of the *Union List of Manuscripts in Canadian Repositories* (Ottawa 1975) and its *Supplements* (1976 and 1977/78) is in order, as is a glance through the index of PAM listings. The records of the Union Bank, for example, which operated an extensive network of branches in the West, are located in Waterloo, and most of the Manitoba Wheat Pool records related to rural communities are now deposited in the Rural Archives, Community Resource Centre, Brandon University.

A more demanding but still valuable approach to local business research is through the advertising and news columns of the local newspaper. Not only will the paper publicize the opening of a business but often it will record its wares and prices and changes in ownership and physical features.

CHAPTER 7

Federal and Provincial Politics

A SURVEY

The history of provincial and national politics has been studied from many vantage points, though rarely from the perspective of local activity and voting patterns. Because emotions, interests, and perspectives are so clearly expressed in election campaigns and party organizations, a study of local politics can be particularly rewarding. Moreover, local analysis may well demonstrate how misleading are histories of political events seen only from the capital city and the party leader's office.

The earliest formal government in this territory was the Hudson's Bay Company's Council of Assiniboia, first appointed in 1835. It was succeeded by several provisional governments during the troubled years of 1869-70. In 1870, with the completion of negotiations to transfer the northwest from the Hudson's Bay Company administration to Canada, a provincial government was established.

The character of provincial politics in Manitoba changed rapidly in succeeding decades. The uneasy partnership between the fur trade and agriculture, between French- and English-speaking citizens, old and new settlers, Metis and Europeans, collapsed in the first decade after Confederation. The tolerant development-oriented atmosphere of the 1880s was presided over by Premier John Norquay (1878-87), who represented the old civilization though he made way for the new. Battles with Ottawa over railways and with the French and Catholics over schools were the hallmarks of the first Liberal administration in the province, led by Thomas Greenway (1888-99). The Macdonald (1899) and Roblin (1900-15) Conservative administrations were distinguished by effective organization in districts settled by Europeans, by the arousal of Imperial sentiment in British settlements, and by considerable sympathy for the farming community, traits which were sufficient to win four elections before scandal brought the government down. Reform movements which affected the status of women, labourers, farmers, and the sale of liquor dominated the first five years of the T.C. Norris Liberal government (1915-20), but were curtailed in the second Norris administration (1920-22), after the indecisive election of 1920. Premier John Bracken (1922-42) restored political stability with his cautious administration of a "Progressive" farmers' government which increasingly dominated the political spectrum and reduced participation in provincial electoral politics. The real upheaval came not with the Stuart Garson (1942-8) and the D.L. Campbell Liberal-Progressive governments (1948-58) after Bracken went to Ottawa, but with the emergency of an aggressive Conservative party under Errick Willis and then Duff Roblin in the 1950s.

Roblin became premier in 1958 and led a pragmatic development-conscious administration for a decade. His chief opposition, the Co-operative Commonwealth Federation (which became the New Democratic Party in 1961), was a product of political protest in the 1920s and 1930s. The CCF had not been absorbed by the Bracken government but had been sustained by labour and socialist movements in North End Winnipeg and in the poorer agricultural regions of the province. The party built a stronger organization in the 1960s and defeated Roblin's successor, Walter Weir (1967-9), with the aid of the popular young leader, Ed Schreyer (1969-77). The Conservatives returned to power under Sterling Lyon in 1977.

Local questions dominated federal elections in the first years after Manitoba joined Confederation, but by 1878 the national political machines of the Reform (Liberal) party and the Liberal-Conservative (Conservative) party were active in the campaign. The two national parties debated provincial rights issues (which level of government should determine railway policy and control public lands) in the 1880s, and economic development remained a focal point in the 1890s, though the provincial schools question also preoccupied politicians. The Roblin-Rogers Conservative organization was able to blame the Laurier government for Manitoba's failure to secure "provincial rights" concessions, including the Hudson Bay Railway, boundary extension, and control of public lands, and, with its strong campaign team, held the province for the party until Borden's victory in 1911. Then, in 1917, the wartime Union Government received a warm welcome from eligible voters. (In this election, it should be noted, "enemy aliens" naturalized after 1902 were disfranchised.) Because they contributed to the rise of farm and labour reform movements after the war, Manitobans helped to destroy the national two-party system between 1919 and 1922.

From the watershed election of 1921, Manitobans consistently elected representatives of Labour and farm parties (most were united in the CCF in 1933) as well as the two old parties and a number of other smaller groups. When the Conservatives named John Diefenbaker as party leader in 1956, however, these divisions were overwhelmed by the rush to support him in 1957 and especially in 1958. This sympathy for the federal Conservatives has remained a significant factor in federal politics in the province through the 1970s.

APPROACHES TO STUDIES OF FEDERAL AND PROVINCIAL POLITICS

The questions to be asked about local activity in provincial and national politics relate principally to electoral results, party organizations, and local opinion on particular issues. These studies can focus on one campaign, on a local theme during a number of campaigns (the Mennonite vote in Springfield constituency, for example, or the impact of the Hudson Bay Railway on The Pas), on the type of local candidate (to determine whether a pattern is evident concerning sex, age, occupation, religion, ethnic group), and on the rise and fall of certain movements (temperance, Patrons of Industry, Social Credit, Progressives). One might attempt to learn whether citizens in certain ethnic groups or religious denominations or geographical areas prefer one party or type of candidate by relating poll results to the census reports where this is possible. One might compare the national reports of election issues, as recounted in historical studies or contemporary accounts (the *Canadian Annual Review* 1900-1938, 1960 to the present contains good summaries) with the local political debates as reported in newspapers and archival collections. One might try to determine the activities of the local political organizations, too, in the hope of discovering for example whether the Roblin-Rogers "machine" was as impressive as was alleged by contemporaries. Finally, one might wish to describe in detail the leadership of the local party organizations; perhaps one group of citizens controls a party, and perhaps one interest dominates policy discussion and candidate selection.

SOURCES

Provincial politics in Manitoba are surveyed clearly in a number of historical works, particularly the studies by W.L. Morton, J.A. Jackson, J. Kendle, M.S. Donnelly, and T.E. Peterson. There are many specialized studies as well, ranging from Ph.D dissertations to articles in journals, but only a handful can be cited here.

The primary source material for political studies is extensive. First and foremost, once again, newspapers will be very useful. The reports of the chief electoral officer after each election and by-election, which constitute the official election returns, are also very important. The Manitoba reports have been unusually difficult to obtain in the past, but recent steps have made them more accessible. The 1977 *Statement of Votes*, published as the *Thirty-First General Election 1977: Report of the Chief Electoral Officer* by the Government of Manitoba, contains an excellent summary of information concerning the 1977 election, including popular vote by poll, the legal description of the poll, and electoral expenditures. In addition, this volume contains a summary of the popular vote and results, by constituency, for all general elections since 1870. Finally, the Provincial Library has prepared a microfilm copy of the extant electoral records for the province. These two reels contain most of the poll results for almost every constituency since 1892 and constituency totals for the elections between 1874 and 1892. They do not include descriptions of the polls, however, so a careful analysis of the results cannot rely on this source alone. Rather, until these records are found, we will have to rely on newspaper descriptions of the polls. The Provincial Archives of Manitoba holds a copy of the 1870 electoral results, which records the choice of every voter in the province.

Careful transcriptions of the election results should be taken and lodged in a local library or repository for future use, for these are the bread and butter of political study. Wherever possible, be sure to determine the boundaries of the constituency in each election, the official number of eligible voters, and franchise restrictions.

There are many collections of documents in the Provincial Archives of Manitoba and in other repositories which are relevant to this kind of study. Whether one chooses to undertake the extensive work of consulting the inventories and examining boxes of letters and papers will depend on the nature of the project and the time available. The collections in PAM concerning the Lieutenant Governors, Premiers, and Public Life (respectively MG 12, 13, 14) will be most relevant.

To obtain the perspective of ethnic voters, the student should consult ethnic newspapers such as *Der Nordwesten, Heimskringla,* and so on. (See D.M. Loveridge, *A Historical Directory of Manitoba Newspapers, 1859-1978.*)

Federal politics in Manitoba can be studied with the aid of J.M. Beck's *Pendulum of Power,* a survey of the campaigns and results of the general elections from 1867 to 1965. Beck's brief chapters on the national issues and significant voting trends provide a context for research into local organizational and electoral history, but there are dozens of other sources which also refer to Manitoba (see bibliography). The complete returns for every general election and by-election, by electoral district, including notices of Grant of a Poll for general elections since 1945 (this describes the geographical limits of each polling division), and lists of electors for each general election since 1935, are available on microfilm at the Public Archives of Canada and the Office of the Chief Electoral Officer, Ottawa. The PAC will sell copies of these films. Records of poll-by-poll results for every election, without poll boundaries, are also printed in the reports of the Chief Electoral Officer, which are included in the Sessional Papers of the House of Commons. Since these records do not list the party affiliation of the candidates, one must also consult the *Canadian Parliamentary Guide*, a helpful but not infallible directory to each constituency. See also "Federal election maps," *Canadian Cartographer 9:1* (1972).

CHAPTER 8

Local Government

A SURVEY

The story of local government can hardly be omitted from a study of local history. In Canada, the provinces are responsible for organizing local governments — whether townships, municipalities, or counties. The first counties were established in Manitoba in 1871. Two years later a general municipal system was set up. Under this legislation a municipality could be organized whenever two-thirds of the adult male householders of an area petitioned for it. Once organized, the municipality could then pass by-laws respecting roads, fire protection, health standards, and so forth but its powers of taxation were very limited.

In the years 1875-83 a county system based on the Ontario model was tried, and in the first eight years of operation six counties were organized. An 1879 bill providing for the incorporation of villages and towns led to the creation of legal corporations in Emerson (1879) and Portage la Prairie (1881). By this statute, a large group of citizens from a comparatively densely populated area with a sufficient taxable assessment could petition to have their community incorporated. Though the number of petitioners and the taxable assessment have been revised over the years, this procedure remains unchanged.

Larger more centralized counties were tried in 1883. These twenty-six counties were grouped into three judicial districts and a judicial district board was used to co-ordinate municipal actions within each district. This centralized system, which failed mainly because of the sparse population and the distances involved, was modified in 1886 by the introduction of the office of Municipal Commissioner and smaller rural municipalities. This has been retained with few alterations, though the Municipal Commissioner was replaced by a Department of Municipal Affairs in 1953.

The basic unit of local government in Manitoba is the council. In towns and villages the council is headed by a mayor; in rural municipalities by a reeve. In general, a person can stand for election only if he or she has reached the legal age, is a taxpayer with no taxes in arrears, has no criminal record, has no occupational affiliation with municipal government or the judiciary, and is not a member of Parliament. The council is responsible for vital services such as police and fire protection, and it manages such matters as street lighting, sewer and water works, street paving, weed control, garbage collection, and the provision of recreational facilities. In co-operation with the local Board of Trade or Chamber of Commerce, a council may try to assist the economic development of a community by wooing industries and businesses.

To pay for these services, the council collects revenues. These take many forms, ranging from parking fines to business licences, but most important among them is the tax on real property (including all land, buildings, and improvements within the community's corporate limits). Periodically, the value of all real property is reassessed and taxes are revised accordingly. From this tax, communities have traditionally derived the funds necessary for civic improvements. In recent years, however, the cost of improvements has risen so fast that property tax revenues are no longer adequate to cover them. This has led to borrowing, usually through the sale of bonds or debentures, to pay for major capital expenditures. Grants from the two senior governments are also available for certain projects.

APPROACHES TO THE STUDY OF LOCAL GOVERNMENT

The membership of the local council, as is the case with any representative government, can be studied with profit. What is its composition by sex, age, ethnic group, religion, occupation? Has it changed over the years? How can these changes or the lack of changes be explained?

The issues which come before council are also revealing. Is there a pattern in the issues? Is there change over time and, if so, why? If there are recorded votes on these issues, is it possible to explain the divisions within the group of councillors?

Finally, one can examine the role of the council in the development of the district. Did the council adopt policies which affected the growth and prosperity of the town? How were the decisions reached?

SOURCES

The best source of information about the local government of your community or municipality is the council's records. A telephone call to the local secretary-treasurer of the council should reveal whether these records are available. At the same time you might enquire about the local tax rolls. Taken together, these two sources can provide an extremely valuable, if somewhat discursive, history of social and financial development. Next in importance will be the local newspaper, which customarily reports on council meetings. Should council records be missing, you can always resort to previous local histories. These will generally supply enough information to form a skeleton history of the council. For statistical information on the municipality, consult the annual publication (1953-   ) of the Department of Municipal Affairs, called *Statistical Information Respecting the Municipalities of the Province of Manitoba and the Metropolitan Corporation of Greater Winnipeg.* For incorporated centres with populations over 1,000, try a publication called *Canadian Municipal Financial Statistics* (1967-   ), issued by the Bureau of Municipal Research. The journal *Western Municipal News* (1906-   , monthly to 1966) is also helpful. Finally, consult Manitoba Sessional Papers, Department of Municipal Commissioner, 1905-15. All of this material is available in the Legislative Library.

For information on prominent local citizens, consult the obituary files of newspapers and the biographical files and scrapbooks at the Legislative Library.

CHAPTER 9

Social Studies

A SURVEY

The examination of the physical, economic, and political features of your community will give you a clear picture of its "skeleton" but will not tell the story of ordinary people doing ordinary things that we usually perceive as "real life." This variety of history is concerned with the activities of every day: the work we do, how we spend our spare time, and the clubs or associations we support. Then, too, the physical expression of our past — buildings, dress, ornaments, and furniture — also help to explain and illustrate what we are like. The basic social unit in the province, the family, has had a profound influence on all of us and thus it, too, can be studied with profit. Each of these categories (work, leisure, voluntary associations, material history, architecture, family history) represents an approach to local social studies which will take the student behind the categories of the census or the soil chart to the flesh and blood of everyday life.

The world of work has an obvious importance in any community. The work experience of a particular tradesman may well have been lost with the passing of years; yet, once appreciated, it may explain a great deal about a way of life. Many workers held a number of jobs in their lifetime and thus picked up numerous skills. Some rose in status and learned the politics of the workplace from several vantage points. Still others were constantly on the move, changing jobs and homes with apparent abandon. How did one learn a new skill or occupation and how did another adapt to a new language on the job? Work and workplaces are often keenly remembered and thus make ideal subjects for interviews; and studies of jobs and working conditions make fascinating topics for research.

Leisure activities in this province can become objects of study if we can look beyond the minutes of club meetings to discover the vitality and role and attraction of the sport or pastime. The changes in literary associations, the development of music clubs, the hey-day of live theatre, the temperance and revival and labour lectures, formal and informal sporting competitions, the district dance and the tennis group are aspects of social life which can be studied with profit. The history of these activities, again, should focus on why they took place, who participated or joined the audience, and what factors influenced their development. Why, for example, did Souris find lacrosse so attractive in 1887-89 and again in 1903-05? What happened to the popularity of the game? Why did Holland have a Drama Society and a Literary or Debating Society, and what happened at the meetings of each?

The number of clubs and voluntary associations that have existed in small towns and rural districts is now legendary; one can only wonder that citizens found time to get from one meeting to the next. Fraternal organizations like the Masonic Order, business groups like the Board of Trade, youth leagues like Boy Scouts and Girl Guides, service committees like the Hospital Guild and the Library Executive, ethnic brotherhoods like the Ukrainian National Federation, and farm groups like 4-H and the Seed Club could co-exist in one district. In addition, specific events like the centennial celebrations, a Royal visit, or a natural disaster would find a response in special groups whose sole purpose was to rise to the needs of the occasion and then disappear, proof having been given that the community was as able and proud as any other. Why did the groups begin? What did they do? Who was active in their direction and support? If they have disappeared, why did they not survive? Can one generalize about the group by its nationality, place of residence, or income? Were the subjects of the Women's Institute sessions indicative of an attitude to woman's role in the community and family? What was the attitude to sports? to cultural activites? to occupational education such as stock-growing clubs?

Historians are much more comfortable with records of the past which appear in written form than with records in the shape of a chair or a morning coat. As a result, except for the occasional descriptive passage employed for "local colour," objects do not play a large part in the historian's attempt to re-create or analyse past society. But the material remains of earlier times do provide an important insight into other cultures, as a visit to any effective museum display or historic site will demonstrate. The use of artifacts for the study of local history can provide research projects in a wide range of social and cultural questions.

The student of "material history" starts with an examination of the object and a series of questions about its origin and use. ["Introduction" to

Material History Bulletin, National Museum of Man Mercury Series No. 15, Ottawa 1976] For example, in looking at a sideboard, you may wonder where it was made, how it was constructed, and what the working conditions were in the shop. You could compare the style to earlier and later design in this and other regions. And you might find out who owned it to determine the diffusion of style or to suggest the influence of class or social or cultural factors in home furnishings. This same approach can be taken to other material remains of a civilization, including glass, pottery, jewellery, silverwork, clothing, weaving, quilting, and so on.

A related and yet distinct approach to local history is the study of architecture. Again, social and economic developments will often be readily apparent from the dates of construction of buildings or from the style and materials employed. The pattern and distribution of types of building (commercial or industrial or residential), may change over a period of years, thereby suggesting changes in transportation systems or shifts in economic fortune. A new route for a highway, for example, can lead to the construction of a series of new buildings along its right-of-way and, thus, the creation of a new "face" for the town. Individual buildings, like other artifacts, can be studied on their own. Materials (local or imported), ornamentation, style, alteration, function, and ownership all can be topics for enquiry.

Family history has been an important part of many published local histories in Manitoba but, for a variety of reasons, these sections have not been as useful as they might have been. Often, these notations on "early pioneers" are not provided in a uniform format; the notes could be made more valuable if they included basic information like dates of birth and death, place of origin (as precisely as possible), date of arrival in Canada and in the district, occupations and places of residence, and similar outlines for children and even grandchildren. These notes should be retained in a local repository for use by students.

Genealogical studies are well developed in Manitoba as a result in particular of the activities of the Manitoba Genealogical Society. If you wish to trace an ancestor or, indeed, any individual, you should contact this group. There are a few obvious places to start your search, however, so you might turn first to the important secondary sources (see bibliography).

Once you have an overview of provincial history and bibliographical aids (including ethnic and local history sources), you might turn to government records and the materials which are noted below.

Genealogy — a search for ancestors and descendants — can be regarded as the first step toward a family history. But as a directory is not a social study, so a family tree is no more than an outline of a family's story. What was life in the household like? What was the role of father, of mother, of the eldest child, of the boys, of the girls? How was money managed, food provided, the holiday celebrated, the vist to grandparents regarded? Where were the crisis points and where the happy times? How were children supposed to be raised?

SOURCES

How can you obtain answers to these questions about clubs and dances and families. Rarely, it must be said, will the minutes of an organization reveal such stories. Newspapers will always provide odd useful bits of material but the items may be difficult to relate to each other and to the wider question. Richer by far are the personal letters, diaries, scrapbooks, and household account books that seem much too personal to be given to an archivist but which may be loaned to a friend. And, here, the much-discussed technique of oral history becomes significant for the study of local history. By working in a small locality, students can walk the lands and streets about which they write and can talk to the subjects of their stories. In most cases, they will be welcomed enthusiastically because of their interest. And the interview sessions provide not only tapes or notes but may bring to light an album or a collection of letters that will help to illuminate the history of a district.

Detailed inquiry into material and architectural history in Canada has begun only in recent years, so the sources for such study in Manitoba are sparse. The Manitoba Museum of Man and Nature, however, can provide assistance in this field. The study of local buildings can begin with the various directories (see appendix 4), and the two series of fire insurance atlases in the PAM, which indicate the site of almost all buildings in the province, including their size and type of construction, for the era of the First World War and for the later 1950s or 1960. The photograph collections in the PAM and local museums will also be invaluable. Mail order catalogues provide a fine introduction to furnishings and material culture and so, too, do the advertisements in newspapers. A free pamphlet issued by Parks Canada, "The Buildings of Canada," by Barbara A. Humphreys and Meredith Sykes (reprinted from Explore Canada, published by *Readers' Digest*), will introduce students to building types and styles but also to the important work of the Canadian Inventory of Historic Buildings, Parks Canada. Their analysis of historic architecture in Manitoba has resulted in extensive computer-organized files on public and private buildings. Write the division with inquiries about their work in a particular area. (The address is 114 Garry Street, Winnipeg).

The PAM contains a number of collections of documents of Women's Institutes, on family histories, and on assorted other societies. The Société historique de Saint-Boniface holds extensive genealogical files on Franco-Manitoban families.

Records of births, marriages, and deaths are administered by the Office of Vital Statistics, Department of Health and Social Development, but are incomplete for the years before 1920. Similar material is available in church records, some of which are housed in the same office, while others are in PAM and yet more can be located through the offices of the churches. (See the Manitoba Genealogical Society for details.) The early census records of Manitoba also supply valuable genealogical information because, from the Hudson's Bay Company census of 1827 to the Dominion of Canada census of 1881, the nominal return (which includes name, age, marital status, and much more) is available. Court records, particularly those of the wills and probate division, can be useful; a central registry of the latter is maintained at the Surrogate Court in Winnipeg. Using the land records can be complicated but the PAC has an alphabetical index to all homestead patentees, 1873-1930, and to settlers' claims from 1870 to 1885 (copies of the latter are at PAM). The land records of the CPR are in the Glenbow-Alberta Institute and of the CNR in its Real Estate Department.

School records, municipal records, military records, and directories can also be used to trace the career or location of individuals. The Cummins Rural Directory Maps, which show the names of landowners throughout the province, were produced in two series, the first ca. 1918 (PAM) and the second ca. 1922 (PAC and on microfilm), and can be very useful though they are not accompanied by an index. For individuals whose presence in the West was associated with the activities of the Hudson's Bay Company, its archives (housed in PAM, with microfilm copies in PAC and the Public Records Office, London England) are an invaluable source of information.

CHAPTER 10

Education

A SURVEY

During the first half of the nineteenth century, schools were organized by religious denominations in the Red River settlement and, to a limited degree, in the smaller fur trade settlements. After Manitoba entered Confederation in 1870, and settlers moved beyond the limits of the Red River parishes, new arrangements for schools became necessary. The Public School Act of 1871 established a denominational school system comprised of twenty-four school districts, twelve Catholic and twelve Protestant, in accordance with the division of the population. Each school district was governed by a board of trustees which was responsible for providing school facilities and hiring teachers. This dual school system was supported by public funds with equal grants to both Protestant and Catholic institutions.

Over the next two decades extensive changes were made in the system chiefly as a result of the dramatic shift in population in favour of an English-speaking and Protestant majority. The increased population brought demands for more schools, the expansion of teacher training and secondary school facilities. It also resulted in some debate over the merits of a dual school system based on religious differences. The result of these factors was the passage of the Public Schools Act and An Act Respecting the Department of Education in the legislative session of 1890. The latter created an Education Department and gave it broad powers over provincial teachers and curricula. The revised Public School Act effectively turned control of the educational system over to the province's English-speaking Protestant population by replacing the dual system with a single "non-denominational" system. Roman Catholics and members of some other denominations opposed this discriminatory legislation and, despite improvements in the educational process in succeeding years, including statutory provision for secondary schools, Roman Catholic and French discontent could not be assuaged.

Finally, in 1897, by the so-called Laurier-Greenway compromise, the Manitoba government agreed to institute bilingual instruction in schools with ten or more pupils whose first language was not English, and to permit religious instruction for those who desired it at the end of the school day. This measure did much to mitigate the religious and ethnic conflict, but it also created other problems, particularly because one phrase in the compromise permitted instruction in English and any other language, and not just in English and French. The demands of other ethnic groups for such instruction alarmed the government, which was forced to provide teacher training in many languages and in several centres outside Winnipeg — Brandon, Portage la Prairie, Dauphin and Manitou.

The education system functioned on this multilingual basis for two decades. Continuing immigration created a shortage of trained teachers, however, and this, combined with the increasing concern of the English-speaking majority for their institutions, produced a campaign against the use of languages other than English in the schools. The provincial government attempted to settle the issue in 1916 when it abolished all bilingual schools, including those of the Franco-Manitobans. This expedient eliminated the confusion inherent in the 1897 compromise, but it did nothing to alleviate the language problem.

The next four decades were a period of gradual change in Manitoba's education system. Elementary, secondary, and post-secondary education was extended. Teacher training and special education facilities were vastly improved. Between 1917 and 1958 the number of teachers more than doubled, and teacher training facilities were centralized in Winnipeg and Brandon. The curriculum was revised in important respects. The process of school consolidation, which was most significant for rural Manitobans, began in the first decade of the century and proceeded apace. By 1924 all schools with an average attendance of less than five pupils were closed. This process continued slowly, until in the late 1950s the government made a concerted effort to consolidate schools and school districts. In rural Manitoba almost all small schools were closed and students were bussed to larger schools usually in town. With some modifications, this remains the educational pattern in most of the province. Though the changes might seem matters for congratulation, one can question the effectiveness of the school system, too, and ask whether it fulfilled local needs or provided the best possible education.

The last half-century has also been marked by a trend to decentralization of authority over education. The end of central departmental examinations and the development of local control over curriculum have led to greater diversity in school programmes and have been accompanied by a lower school-leaving rate in high schools. These years have also seen a progressively greater emphasis on Canadian studies in the classroom and, more recently, on ethnic and native studies. Industrial and vocational education have been popular in certain periods, and agricultural, co-operative, labour, and women's studies have also received support at different times.

APPROACHES TO THE STUDY OF LOCAL EDUCATION

The history of a school, like that of a church, can be written on several levels. The first, the history of the institution, will focus upon such formal matters as the construction of buildings, local finances, the election of school board members, the selection of teachers, and the numbers of pupils and courses.

The second, the social history of the system, will seek out the attitudes of both pupils and teachers to education and to their school. What was the origin of the school? Were there local battles over denominational and language questions? Did the school have military training and domestic arts and team sports? If these were issues, what were the attitudes to them? Were there patriotic exercises at the school? Was there a school garden and, if so, why was it there? When and how was the first secondary school founded? What was the local response to school consolidation? What was the local record in provincial scholarship competitions? What rules have been established for student dress and behaviour? How have they changed? Who made the rules? Have there been rules for the dress and behaviour of teachers? Have they changed? Who made these rules? What did parents want or expect of teacher and student? Did the plans of parents coincide with those of the school board and the curriculum planners? What were the students being prepared for? Were boys and girls treated differently?

SOURCES

Encompassing most of the period since Manitoba was founded are the Annual Reports of the Board, later the Department, of Education. They contain general statistics on provincial education, curricula, reports on teacher training and special education facilities, lists of scholarship winners and principals, and school inspector reports by Inspectoral Division.

Mary B. Perfect has prepared a list of all the rural schools and school districts in the province with their dates of formation which is available as an M.Ed. thesis in the Faculty of Education Library, University of Manitoba. An important introduction to the attitudes of teachers and educational officials is available in their journals. Both the *Educational Journal of Western Canada* 1899-1903, and *The Western School Journal* 1906-38, have been indexed (see bibliography). The provincial teachers' bulletin (the *MTF Bulletin*, 1920-24, and *Manitoba Teacher*, 1924-present), and the trustee's bulletin are also helpful. These journals also contain material on school construction and organization.

The school register can provide valuable insights into the district society. Local patterns of attendance might be related to income and ethnic group of the family, for example, in order to discover if there are general trends in school performance and graduation. Which students dropped out and when did they do so? The registers, if preserved, would be in the school board office or, in rarer cases, in the school building.

Another approach to a more specific topic which might be suitable in high school classes is the study of school yearbooks. Some collections of these volumes, usually located in the school library and in family records, date back to the late nineteenth century. They give class and graduation lists and also describe such extracurricular activities as sports and drama and music.

Minutes of school board meetings are usually carefully preserved in school district offices and provide an insight not only into the institutional history of building construction and teacher salaries but also into the issues which have prompted local debate such as consolidation and language instruction.

The Provincial Library maintains a scrapbook and clipping file on education and the provincial Department of Education library has a variety of resources, including the Annual Reports, departmental examinations, and some old textbooks. The Faculty of Education Library, University of Manitoba, has a collection of theses on education which includes a number of studies of specific localities, including Norwood, Hamiota, Evergreen, Mystery Lake, and Morris-Macdonald. Both PAM and the Department Library hold microfilm copies of the Half Yearly Reports of Schools and School Districts, 1915-66. The PAM also has numerous school division records (for example, Agassiz, Euclid, St. Pierre, Stonewall), and the papers of the Provincial Trustees (43 feet).

For more advanced approaches to the topic consult Asa Briggs, "The Study of the History of Eduction," *History of Education* 1:1 (Jan. 1972).

CHAPTER 11

Religion

A SURVEY

As a place of worship, a source of fellowship, a bastion of particular cultures, a vehicle of assimilation or social change, and a shelter in time of distress, the local church occupied a powerful position in community life during Manitoba's first century. When its members were united, the church was a source of comfort and stability. But when conflicts erupted — over the nature of the service, the role of the pastor, or the behaviour of adherents — the church could actually drive or lead members out of the community in search of new homes. Differences of opinion within churches could become angry confrontations, but a conflict between denominations was often the source of a deeper and longer-lasting bitterness. Thus, whether as a source of strength or, more rarely, as the cause of dissatisfaction, churches were central to the daily round of activities in Manitoba.

APPROACHES TO RELIGIOUS STUDIES

The history of a local church can be written along the lines of any institutional study, encompassing the formal governmental structure, the details of finance and construction and furnishing, and the incumbents in the offices of minister and congregational or parish executives. But this, as was suggested above, is only one aspect of the church's existence, and not the most important, at that. Church members were often active in public affairs as spokesmen for their fellows, for example, advocating support for the temperance movement or school legislation or the store closing by-law. What were their arguments and how were they expressed? Churches often had extensive programmes of activities throughout the week and in every season. Who participated in the children's club, the young adults' group or the study session and what were the goals of each? What role did the church play in the preservation or propagation of cultural values? What was the reaction of the Protestant churches to the influx of Catholic and Orthodox settlers? Did the local churches provide charitable assistance? For whom? Finally, what were the teachings of the church, its criticisms of local society and its ideals?

SOURCES

Sources for the study of church history are widely dispersed. One obvious means of learning about church activities, however, is the local newspaper. A second is the collection of records of the local congregation. Records of baptisms, confirmations, marriages and burials are often available to students of history. The minutes of various church boards and organizations are also kept. Hymnaries and children's religious lessons can provide interesting insights into the ideas of a denomination. Ministers' sermons, too, are sometimes stored in these collections. Financial records do not usually contain much detail, but they do suggest how funds were allocated if not where they came from. The third important source is the provincial, national, or denominational archive for the church in question. These vary widely in usefulness and accessibility but some are very rich in their resources.

The United Church Archives in the University of Winnipeg Library holds the minutes for many individual Methodist and Presbyterian churches since the 1880s, for the districts (or regional governing boards), for the Manitoba conference of the Methodist church, and for comparable bodies in the Presbyterian church (presbytery and synod). It also contains many copies of church magazines and newpapers and pamphlets from the period prior to 1925. Assorted records of United Church congregations are also stored here. A list of these holdings, prepared by W.H. Brooks, is available at the university library. The PAM also holds the records of some local churches and of a number of ministers in these denominations. A microfilm copy of the Methodist newspaper, *The Christian Guardian*, is stored in St. Paul's College Library, University of Manitoba.

The Archives of the Ecclesiastical Province of Rupert's Land, Church of England, 1804-1964 (6 feet), including correspondence and reports, is located in the PAM, as are the papers of several religious leaders. The great collection of Church Missionary Society papers, 1821-1924 (48 reels of microfilm), is also available there and so, too, are nineteenth century parish registers of baptisms, marriage and burials.

A Mennonite Heritage Centre, which contains a rich archival collection, has been built on the campus of the Canadian Mennonite Bible College. Other materials related to this group are discussed in two recent articles in

Mennonite Life by Ernest J. Dyck, "Resources on Mennonite History in the Public Archives of Canada" 30:4 (1975) and 31 (1976).

La Société historique de Saint-Boniface, and the Archiepiscopal Archives of Saint Boniface and of the Archdiocese of Winnipeg contain many records concerning the Roman and Ukrainian Catholic Church in the West. The PAM also contains a few Roman Catholic records.

The Western Canada Jewish Historical Society should be contacted for information concerning Jewish synagogues and members of the Jewish community. The society maintains an inventory of manuscripts and published sources which includes information on Jews in such towns as Bender Hamlet as well as on many individuals and associations.

Unitarian church records are rare, but a few are located in the PAM.

An extensive collection of Lutheran Church records for the Interlake area has been housed in the PAM.

The records of the Ukrainian churches, whether Greek Orthodox or Catholic, are scattered. Some remain with the local priest while others have been transferred to central repositories or have been destroyed. The Consistory of the Ukrainian Greek Orthodox Church (9 St. John's Avenue, Winnipeg), does contain an assortment of parish records, as does the Consistory of the Ukrainian Catholic Church (St. Vladimir and Olga Cathedral, Winnipeg). A number of private collections are also valuable. It would be wise to consult the Ukrainian Cultural and Educational Centre, Winnipeg, and St. Andrew's College, University of Manitoba, for guidance in this area.

Many ministers have written memoirs, some of which have been published while others remain in manuscript form in the ecclesiastical or provincial archives. The once-numerous church-run or church-affiliated journals provide an insight into church activities which is available in few other sources. Copies are often available in specialized collections though complete runs are rare.

Finally, one unusually interesting source of material on churches is the student journal, magazine, or newspaper. Back issues of the *St. John's College Magazine* or *Vox Wesleyana*, for example, provide rich introductions to the attitudes and activities of entire generations of ministers.

A list of church archives is included in Appendix 5.

CHAPTER 12

Other Professions: Law, Medicine, and Social Services

A SURVEY

The history of law, medicine, and social services in Manitoba has not been chronicled in detail, so this chapter will present a brief introduction to the topic. The role of doctors and hospitals in those districts fortunate enough to have such services will be obvious. The legal system, through the police and the courts, touches every community. Social services and the public health system, developments of the twentieth century, now reach many communities in the province and thus play a part in the history of local society.

The history of legal institutions in Manitoba has been characterized as a history of "substantial justice" by Dale and Lee Gibson. It is unlikely that local historians will overturn that view, but they may add a number of nuances to the story. One might expect that the bench and the legal profession were dominated by members of French-Canadian or Anglo-Saxon parentage during the province's first seventy-five years, and that they shared the social and political assumptions of the urban commercial leaders. One might predict that crimes against property and crimes involving drink predominated in Manitoba's first half-century, and have been supplemented by crimes of violence against persons and those involving motor vehicles in recent decades. One might suppose that citizens in the dock would be more often poor than rich, ethnic or native than Anglo-Saxon, graduates of grade school rather than university. But answers to these questions must await further study.

SOURCES

The study of legal institutions, law-breaking, and police activity in Manitoba has not received much attention and, aside from the pioneering work of Roy Stubbs and Dale and Lee Gibson, little has been published. The collection and preservation of records has now begun, however, so the field is likely to attract more attention in the near future.

The establishment of the Archives of Western Canadian Legal History at the School of Law, University of Manitoba, provides one reason for optimism. Under the supervision of Professor R.D. Gibson, a biographical index has been created which contains references to many of the lawyers who practised in Manitoba and a few who practised in the other prairie provinces. The archive also contains the papers of the Law Society of Manitoba from the late nineteenth century, including the Society's scrapbooks on legal matters. The remainder of its collection is the product of gifts and discoveries, including some Emerson police records and a few items on the Manitoba Provincial Police.

The Public Archives of Manitoba also holds some items concerning law and police, chief amongst which are the records of the Quarterly Court of Assiniboia and the prisoner records of several jails. The PAC has the records of the North-West, later Royal Canadian, Mounted Police, but much of this material is closed to the public. An inventory of this group is available free of charge from the PAC.

Several directories provide lists of lawyers and maps of the court circuits. The *Canadian Law List* (published annually since 1883) and the *Canadian Legal Directory* (an annual since 1911) will outline the judicial districts, the judges of the various courts, and the lawyers in each town. Those lawyers who have been admitted to the Manitoba bar are also listed in the records of the Law Society of Manitoba. The Society keeps its members informed of gossip and news in the profession with its *Manitoba Bar News*, (1928-29 bi-monthly; 1929 to the present monthly).

One source of information concerning court proceedings is the published account of a case which appears in a law report. These journals do not report on every case, by any means, but those which affect the law or have unusual features will usually be noted in summary form. The western Canadian journals include: *Western Law Times*, ed. Archer Martin (1890/1-1895 annual), the *Manitoba Law Journal* or *Manitoba Reports* (1883/4-1962 annual), and *Western Weekly Reports* (1911 to the present, annual). They are available at the Law Library, University of Manitoba, and some are also housed in the larger Court House libraries and the Legislative Library.

There are several other sources of information which may be of value. Records of the local police force are sometimes maintained in the police station, the court house, or in town council files. Case records from individual courts can be a gold mine of material on local society but, for the most part, they have never been organized for the use of research students. Write a letter of inquiry to the Clerk of Court in your district, and follow with a personal visit to decide whether the job of sorting the dusty boxes into some order is worth the time. Finally, the Department of the Attorney-General, Manitoba, holds records on the establishment of courts and on a number of special legal matters but, again, it is necessary to ask permission to use this material and it has not been organized for researchers.

The story of public health services is also yet to be told. The Provincial Archives does, however, house the records of the Manitoba Department of Health and Welfare (file RG 5 E1), which include information on such topics as public-health nursing, the Manitoba Sanitorium, the activities of the public welfare commission, and the Brandon Mental Hospital. One might also seek information on the informal predecessors of these government agencies, such as the midwife, the Mountie's wife, the patent medicine salesman, and the itinerant dentist. The best introduction to social services in Manitoba is "Progressive Social Policy in Manitoba, 1915-1939," a thesis prepared for the School of Social Work of the University of Manitoba by Aleda Turnbull, which can be consulted at the Dafoe Library.

The Manitoba Hospital Organization, 377 Colony Street, Winnipeg, maintains historical files on each of its 150 member facilities. The files, which vary in usefulness, are open to the public. Perhaps the best insight into the provision of medical facilities can be obtained in the files of the local hospital or clinic; here, personal approaches to the administrator or board would necessarily precede research.

The papers of the College of Physicians and Surgeons of Manitoba (16 feet) are deposited at the PAM. The annual reports of the government departments in each area are also rich in information concerning new programmes as well as the details of administration.

CHAPTER 13

Special Themes in Manitoba Historical Studies

ARCHAEOLOGY

Archaeology is a technique of studying the past using the material remains of the culture. In Manitoba, archaeologists have concentrated on the period between the retreat of the glaciers, about ten thousand years ago, and the beginning of the fur trade.

Though local historians may wish to examine local material from the epoch prior to the seventeenth century, it is a very complex undertaking requiring guidance from professional archaeologists. A series of leaflets on Manitoba archaeology, published by the Historic Resources Branch of the provincial Department of Cultural Affairs and Historical Resources should also be consulted at an early stage. Do resist the temptation to dig up the district's pre-history on your own; legal as well as academic disapproval await the unwary amateur. You will render a greater service by reporting any discovery of evidence of past human habitation to the Provincial Archaeologist, Historic Resources Branch, Government of Manitoba. This person is available for consultation on such matters and is also prepared to assist in the preparation of local pre-history studies.

SINGLE-ENTERPRISE COMMUNITIES

The main difference between the "typical" prairie town and the single-enterprise community, or company town, is the dominant position the company holds in the social and economic life of the community. The town that grew as a service centre for neighbouring farmers usually relies on professionals, business people, and farmers for leadership. In the single-enterprise town, the same people (doctors, storekeepers, teachers, etc.) may be active in community affairs, but their influence is overshadowed by the company — whether it is a privately owned mine, a railway, or a government-owned power plant. The fortunes of the company will be reflected in the growth of the town, just as its daily and seasonal timetable will determine the daily and seasonal rhythms of town activities.

The history of the town must also be a history of the company. Access to the records of the company is therefore essential (see R.S. Lucas, *Minetown, Milltown, Railtown*). A very helpful introduction to single-enterprise communities is provided by the Northern Affairs office of Planning and Policy Development, which has prepared "Community Profiles" for sixty-five towns or settlements in northern Manitoba.

NATIVE STUDIES

In 1700, people of the Cree, Assiniboine, Ojibway, Chipewyan, and Inuit (Eskimo) cultures spent at least part of each year in what is now Manitoba. The area was also visited by bands of Sioux. The economies of these peoples, originally based on hunting and fishing, were increasingly adapted to trade with Europeans. The native inhabitants welcomed the traders and whalers and came to depend upon European guns, traps, knives, blankets, kettles, and other material goods.

By mid-century, in the 1740s and early 1750s, they had the advantage of a competitive market, for both the Hudson's Bay Company and the men of New France sought to win their trade. Competition remained intense in the half-century after the fall of New France, especially in the years after the formation of the North-West Company (1783-1821) and the New North-West Company (1798-1804). Networks of posts were established in Manitoba and across the western interior. This expansion of the trading system coincided with the increased importation of horses from southwestern America and the greater availability of guns from the British and Canadians. Such changes greatly affected the native way of life. Among the changes in Manitoba could be numbered the emergence of a distinct Plains (as opposed to Woods and Swampy) Cree culture which shared elements with the culture of the Assiniboine and Blackfoot and other Plains people (including the Sun Dance and an increased reliance on the buffalo). Henceforth, rather than travel by canoe to Hudson Bay on an annual trading expedition, these Plains Cree, like the Assiniboine, would hunt buffalo and provide pemmican to the company posts in exchange for guns and other trade goods. At this time, too, the Cree and Ojibway moved into central and western Manitoba and beyond. Other significant changes included the growing number of offspring of marriages between Europeans and natives; the establishment of native settlements around a number of trading posts; and the removal of Chipewyans from territory near Hudson Bay into the interior along the Churchill River system.

The next half-century saw even more rapid change in native society. The merger of the North-West Company into the Hudson's Bay Company in 1821 re-established monopoly control in the Manitoba trade for nearly three decades but, by the end of the 1840s, the company had to acknowledge that private traders could also operate in this territory. The establishment of this "free trade" was a boon to the growing Metis communities at Red River, Pembina and White Horse Plains. The Metis were an important new factor in western society because they acted as a buffer between European and Indian and because as neither native nor newcomer, they complicated local political arrangements. The first half of the nineteenth century was also marked by the arrival of Roman Catholic, Anglican, and Methodist missionaries who established churches and schools at a number of points in the region. During the 1860s and 1870s as outsiders moved into western America on both sides of the forty-ninth parallel, increasing numbers of Sioux migrated to Manitoba from adjacent areas in the United States. But the most significant aspect of the changing times for natives in southern Manitoba was the disappearance of the buffalo from their lands. Their hunts now extended farther to the south and west and met with mixed results.

Within five years of Manitoba's entry into Confederation in 1870, most of the Indians living inside the present-day boundaries of the province, had been brought under Dominion treaties. (These were similar in some respects to the treaty between Lord Selkirk and the Indians signed in 1817.) The Dominion treaty negotiations acknowledged native claims to the land and extinguished them in exchange for an annual payment of money and the guarantee of protection. The treaties also included promises of reserves of land for each "band" (a fixed area would be set aside according to the population), and a range of additional promises, such as a medicine kit, a new suit of clothing or a carriage, which varied with the bargaining at the meeting. Though most Indians were covered by the treaties, the Metis, whether French or English-speaking, accepted a separate arrangement by which they claimed a land grant from the Dominion.

The way of life of the native peoples in Manitoba changed dramatically after 1870. In the south, the rapid extinction of buffalo and the spread of settlement meant that the native people had to learn how to make their living by farming or accept an existence at the margin of the incoming civilization. In the north, Indians could still live off the fur trade and the hunt. Both northern and southern natives, however, had to deal with the Dominion authorities through the regulations of the Indian Act (1876). The federal government's insistence on the election of band chiefs and subsequent control of band policy undercut native political traditions. The suppression of the Sun dance removed a vital element in plains culture and served as a blunt reminder of

Dominion authority. Later, the lack of programmes for economic development, the annexation of Indian reserve lands for the settlers' land market, and poor educational and medical services compounded the problems of poverty. The churches brought some benefits to the natives, including schools and medical care, but for the most part they were unequal to the immense task they had set themselves.

This situation began to change after the Second World War when the federal government assumed full responsibility for native education and health care and started to upgrade standards and expand services in both areas. This, combined with the impact of modern communications systems, encouraged some Indians to work for new political objectives.

The decline of the fur trade, the expansion of the welfare state, and such documents as the *Hawthorn Report* (1964) and the federal white paper, *Statement of the Government of Canada on Indian Policy* (1969) have stimulated Indians to organize their own associations for the attainment of political, economic, and social change (see bibliography). The migration of Indians into the cities of the province has also accelerated sharply in the past three decades. It is difficult to assess the effects of this movement on native communities and on the cities themselves, although it has certainly altered the lives of the individuals who have made the step.

SOURCES

The most remarkable source for native history in the province is the archive of the Hudson's Bay Company, located in the PAM. The so-called "post journals," records of trade and other activity maintained by company officers at each trading post, contain information on a great range of topics, from population to hunting territories to trade relationships. It is not easy, however, to divine the implications of the bald business details contained in these files, so such study should usually be undertaken only with professional supervision.

The records of church missions are similarly useful because they provide the perspective of priest or minister upon the movements and activities of particular groups of natives. The files of the Church Missionary Society of the Anglican Church (PAM, microfilm) and the records of the various Roman Catholic and Methodist missions are especially extensive (see appendix 5).

The most important source of information for the settlement period is the Annual Report of the Department of Indian Affairs. Beginning in 1881, these reports initially contained the observations of the Department's Indian Agents, and detailed the population, location, and activities of each band of Indians. Later, the post of Agent was abolished and the reports recorded only a handful of statistics about the various reserves, including such items as land acreages, crops, educational facilities, religious affiliations, and populations. These key reports were issued in Canada Sessional Papers from 1881 to 1924, then as the departmental reports of the Department of Indian Affairs (1924-36), of the Department of Mines and Resources, Indian Affairs Branch (1937-49), of the Department of Citizenship and Immigration, Indian Affairs Branch (1950-66), and finally of the Department of Indian Affairs and Northern Development (1967 to the present). On the question of population, the National Indian Brotherhood of Canada has compiled a useful item entitled "Registered Indian Population, Canada, 1865-1972". This is available from the National Indian Brotherhood, 100-102 Bank Street, Ottawa, Ontario.

Regarding the treaty period, two sources in particular are very useful. One is *Indian Treaties and Surrenders from 1680 to 1890* (3 vols., 1905 and 1912), which gives the complete texts of the treaties signed in Canada up to 1890. The second source is Alexander Morris, *The Treaties of Canada with the Indians of Manitoba and the North-West Territories* . . . In addition to giving the text of western treaties from 1811 to 1880, Morris also supplies a record of the negotiations of the treaties in which he participated as Indian Commissioner. Although his reports were written from his own point of view and are not unbiased, they are a valuable source of local information.

The papers of the Royal Canadian (North-West) Mounted Police (PAC) also contain material on native people. A full guide to these papers is available free from the PAC.

For many years Indian Affairs has issued a "Schedule of Indian Reserves and Settlements" which indicates the exact locations of reservations, their size, and the band(s) occupying each. Two other publications of the same department are "Atlas of Indian Reserves and Settlements of Canada" (1971), and "Survey of Indian Bands and Reserves in Manitoba" (1971). Adding further to a visual understanding of Manitoba's reserve system is T.R. Weir, *Economic Atlas of Manitoba* (Winnipeg, 1960), which contains a map showing the distribution of native people, population estimates, reserve locations, bands, and linguistic families. See also a publication of PAC, National Map Collection, "Sources for Native Studies: Indian Reserve Maps, Prairie Provinces, 1817-1967."

If these sources prove unprofitable, consult the "Catalogue of Statistical Data Stored in the Program Reference Centre" of the Department of Indian Affairs and Northern Development. Recent sources concerning almost all aspects of native life may also be found in Thomas S. Abler, *A Canadian Indian Bibliography,* and Don Whiteside, *Aboriginal People: A Selected Bibliography* (Ottawa, 1973). The basic guide to earlier literature is G.P.

Murdock, *Ethnographic Bibliography of North America*, 3rd ed. (New Haven,1960).

The Public Records Division (PAC) has published a guide to records relating to Indian affairs in its domain. The huge collection of records from the Department of Indian Affairs is thus more or less open to research, if one has the stamina to investigate the index system of each section of the collection. The largest portion of the records concerning Manitoba is contained in the Central Registry Files (230 feet of documents), but there are other relevant sections, including school files, engineering and construction files and the Manitoba Regional Office files (1939-70). Finally, individual agency files are available for Birtle (paylists 1886-1936); Clandeboye (letters from the agent 1884-97, accounts 1884-1930); Fisher River (paylists and accounts 1875-1940); Brandon Industrial School and Pine Creek Boarding School (admissions and discharges); Manitowapah (paylists, accounts, 1877-1956); Norway House (annuity payments, 1915-25); The Pas (general administration of schools and bands 1912-17, agent's letterbook 1891-2, paylists and accounts); Portage la Prairie (annuity payments, 1884-1936); and St. Peter's Reserve (1907 Commission on Indian Lands).

Study of native history is also conducted by native associations, such as the Manitoba Indian Brotherhood and the Manitoba Metis Federation and by the Departments of Native Studies at the Universities of Manitoba and Brandon.

One important document not to be missed is the report to the Manitoba Department of Agriculture and Immigration entitled "The People of Indian Ancestry in Manitoba: A Social and Economic Study" prepared by J.H. Lagassé.

ETHNIC GROUPS

Students of prairie society have long been interested in the study of ethnic groups, but only in recent years has it become an important part of historical analysis. The result is that some groups have been ignored while others have been treated in detail. The Manitoba Historical Society sponsored a series of volumes on ethnic groups which included works of varying quality on Icelanders, Poles, Mennonites, Hutterites, Ukrainians, and Jews. But despite the growing number of publications which have appeared in recent years, we have much yet to learn.

The two dominant strands of interpretation in this field have focused on the reception of immigrant groups by the larger society and their gradual assimilation into the dominant culture. In the first category, we find that distinctions are drawn between the welcome extended to Icelanders and

Mennonites, who were greeted warmly in the mid-1870s, and the reaction to Ukrainians, who arrived later. Eastern Europeans were seen to have a vastly different cultural background and were considered sufficiently numerous to pose a threat to the established order. A convenient introduction to turn-of-the-century Canadian opinion on the relative merits of the various ethnic groups is provided by J.S. Woodsworth's *Strangers Within Our Gates.* Passing time and changing circumstances affected the standing of some groups and thus, for example, the Germans and other "enemy aliens" knew hard times during the world wars. Finally, concern about the direction of cultural change pushed educational authorities, among others, to make new demands for the assimilation of the newcomers.

Despite the retention of language, national associations, and some cultural programmes, the ethnic groups have in most matters made considerable adjustments to Canadian ways. Therein lies a most important story which can be told only at the local level. Conflicts between traditionalists and modernizers have been waged in every ethnic community. What were the symbols of each side? Where did they take their stand? Much of any ethnic group's life focuses on the "old world." Which aspects of that world continued to be important despite the move to the new land? How were battles between those who maintained their culture and those who preferred to assimilate carried on? Were traditional political or religious divisions (for example, socialist versus capitalist, monarchist versus republican, liberal versus conservative), adapted to the new environment? Was marriage outside the national group or the religion an important issue? If so, what means were used to ensure that the ideal was attained? When did such issues cease to be important, if they are no longer? Was there discrimination — political, economic, or social — against the group? What evidence is available on the issue? If prejudice once existed, has it ceased to be a problem and, if so, when? How was it handled by those who were discriminated against?

SOURCES

Sources for ethnic studies will vary with the group. Ethnic newspapers constitute an invaluable source and should be regarded as one essential avenue of research. See D.M. Loveridge, *A Historical Guide to Manitoba Newspapers*. The most important national archival collection is the Ethnic Archives in the Public Archives of Canada. And, within the Public Records Division of the PAC, the Immigration Branch records are most useful. (Some of these records, on 319 reels of microfilm, are available at the PAM.) These contain, for example, copies of the passenger lists for vessels arriving at Quebec City 1865-99 and Halifax 1881-1900, and registers of Chinese immigrants arriving in Canada 1885-1903. In the same division, one can also find the Dominion Lands Branch records, which include an alphabetical index of the names of those who filed for homestead patents and an incomplete but most extensive "guide to immigration and land settlement sources."

The archives of the Société historique de Saint-Boniface contain, amongst other materials, the records of the Association d'éducation des Canadiens-francais du Manitoba. The Canadian Mennonite Heritage Centre is a large and growing repository, and the Ukrainian Cultural and Educational Centre will probably serve a similar function for that group (though the strongest Ukrainian presence in Canadian scholarship may be the centre at the University of Alberta, Edmonton). The Department of Icelandic Studies at the University of Manitoba is the Canadian focus for Icelandic scholarship. The Western Canada Jewish Historical Society has been mentioned. The Legislative Library has an extensive collection of ethnic newspapers.

A strong case can be made for the argument that ethnic history should first be written by insiders and that this task is especially urgent now when many students still retain language skills and many oldtimers are able to serve as historical informants.

URBAN HISTORY: WINNIPEG AND BRANDON

Cities represent a kind of local community different from the small town or rural district. Students and teachers will find to their pleasure, however, that despite the complexities of this field of inquiry the recent rapid development of urban history and in particular the interest in Winnipeg have produced rich resources upon which they can build their own work. The situation in Brandon is not quite as advanced but several aids to an examination of that city do exist.

There are two approaches to the study of cities, one which emphasizes all historical processes within an urban setting, and a second which concentrates on the city as a unique environment and examines only those topics which are a consequence of the urban setting. In practice, the first approach discusses a wide variety of themes, from business leadership to physical setting and social or political development. The second deals with broad patterns of metropolitan growth (such as the changing functions of a city as it grows from market centre to manufacturing base to transportation hub to finance capital), and with the city-building process (including the influence of such factors as class, ethnic group, economic function, and transportation network upon the location of businesses and residences). A few of these issues can become the topics for student research, as the following pages will suggest. Of these, the most important include the urban physical environment (or topography), transportation systems, the development of neighbourhoods, and the issue of social class.

Winnipeg and Brandon were sites of fur trade activity, and thus the first unit of local study would emphasize the role of natural factors in the selection of trading-post locations. Winnipeg acquired greater prominence in the decade after 1870 when, largely because of its earlier history and the existence of Upper Fort Garry, it became an administrative centre for the region. But the crucial factor in its development, as in the emergence of Brandon, was the choice of the Canadian Pacific Railway route and divisional points in 1880-82. Winnipeg also became the site of the Company's western headquarters and shops. Thereafter, Brandon was assured an important role as the sub-metropolis for western Manitoba. Winnipeg, on the other hand, had even greater potential because, as the first city of the vast western prairies, it had been elevated to national rather than merely regional status. Between 1901 and 1913, the next period of rapid prairie growth, Winnipeg became one of the four great cities of Canada. At that point, however, the city's economy had reached an equilibrium, and, as late as 1945, few new functions had emerged to supplement those it had already served.

It has become a truism to suggest that prairie city governments have been dominated by business and professional interests. Certainly, wholesale and commercial leaders have controlled civic policy-making in Winnipeg and Brandon, but they have done so in the face of consistent criticism and opposition from representatives of the working classes. Class lines in civic government were most obvious after the General Strike of 1919 in Winnipeg; a similar division of outlook could undoubtedly be found in Brandon.

The topography of a city can be a subject of study just as much as the topography of a rural district. In the case of Winnipeg, where there has been a great deal of effort spent on this approach, the results are particularly interesting. The site of the metropolitan district is divided into three segments by the Red and Assiniboine Rivers, a factor which to this day affects the development of neighbourhoods. The city is also divided by railway lines, particularly by the huge Canadian Pacific yards which have been a barrier between north and south since their foundation in the early 1880s. As the functions of the city changed, and urban transportation, especially the street railway and later the automobile, became more efficient, arterial routes permitted the establishment of new suburbs outside the urban core. Table 1 illustrates the pace of suburban growth.

Table 1

Population Growth in Winnipeg and Suburbs, 1901-1971

Suburbs	1901	1911	1921	1931	1941	1951	1961	1971
Assiniboia	357	681	1,024	2,032	1,968	2,663	6,088	— (e)
Charleswood	450	701	869	1,226	1,934	3,680	6,243	12,185
East Kildonan	563	1,488	6,379	9,047	8,350	13,144	27,305	30,150
Fort Garry	730	1,333	2,401	3,926	4,453	8,193	17,528	26,135
North Kildonan (a)	—	—	—	—	1,946	3,222	8,888	17,715
Old Kildonan (b)	—	—	—	—	704	869	1,327	1,865
St. Boniface	2,019	7,483	12,821	16,305	18,157	26,342	37,600	46,750
St. James	257	4,535	11,745	13,903	13,892	19,569	33,977	71,385
St. Vital	585	1,540	3,771	10,402	11,993	18,637	27,269	32,940
Transcona (c)	—	—	4,185	5,747	5,495	6,752	14,248	22,745
Tuxedo (d)	—	—	277	559	777	1,627	1,627	3,260
West Kildonan	668	1,767	4,641	6,132	6,110	10,754	20,077	24,080
Winnipeg	42,340	136,035	179,087	218,785	221,960	235,710	265,429	246,270

NOTES: a) Included with East Kildonan until 1941.
        b) Included with West Kildonan until 1941.
        c) Transcona incorporated in 1921.
        d) Tuxedo incorporated in 1913.
        e) Included with St. James.

Source: *The Metropolitan Development Plan* (Winnipeg, 1968); *Census of Canada, 1971.*

Each of the various functions of the city also became concentrated in certain areas. Commercial establishments were to be found in the central core or along the major streets emanating from it; industrial firms clustered along the rail lines; residential areas were pushed outside the central core and soon they, too, became segregated by class and ethnicity. Some of these features can be seen in city maps. Though the study of Brandon has not yet reached this stage, such an analysis might well produce comparable results.

The focus of urban history should be on the physical environment, the transportation system, neighbourhoods, and perhaps class and ethnic factors in urban life as seen through politics and the economy.

When did a particular district become part of the city? Did it function as a commercial area or was it residential in character? What was the appearance of the main street of the district and has it changed? If the district has been subdivided, why and how did the split take place? The urban transportation system, particularly the street railway and, after cars became important, arterial roads, will have had considerable influence upon the district. The ethnic composition of an area can have an impact upon its schools and upon voting patterns. Material history, particularly the examination of dress, furniture and household items, can produce interesting results in areas that remain ethnically diverse.

SOURCES

The study of Winnipeg has already resulted in a number of valuable works. Of these, the two by Alan F.J. Artibise, *Winnipeg: A Social History of Urban Growth 1874-1914* and *Winnipeg: An Illustrated History* are undoubtedly most useful introductions, as is the beautiful *Atlas of Winnipeg*, prepared by T.R. Weir and Ngok-Wai Lai. From there, the choice is wide. *Gateway City*, edited by Alan Artibise, contains an interesting selection of documents on the city from 1873 to 1913. Two bibliographies are helpful: D. Louise Sloane, Janette M. Roseneder, Marilyn J. Hernandez, *Winnipeg: A Centennial Bibliography;* and P.H. Wichern, *Studies in Winnipeg Politics.* A valuable guide to the evolution of local government and school districts is contained in Wichern, *The Development of Urban Government in the Winnipeg Area.* For a study of local politics, see J.E. Rea, *Politics and Power.* Introductions to spatial analysis are contained in Alan F.J. Artibise and E.H. Dahl, *Winnipeg in Maps*, and Tony J. Kuz, *Winnipeg, 1874-1974.* A general introduction for students is the slide set in the Canada's Visual History Series, A.F.J. Artibise, *Winnipeg: The Growth of a City 1874-1914* (Ottawa, 1974). Perhaps the best means to approach the city, though, is through James Gray's work, especially *The Boy From Winnipeg* and *The Winter Years.*

The secondary sources for the study of Brandon are slight. The best work is a doctoral dissertation by W.L.Clark of Brandon University on the politics of the city. There are a number of local histories, of which the most recent is George Barker, *Brandon: A City*.

Primary sources, in the case of both cities, are still not well-organized. Brandon's Assiniboine Historical Society is working toward the development of city archives, and the City of Winnipeg Archives and Records Control Branch, 380 William Ave., is currently cataloguing its material. The basic sources of most local studies — censuses, maps, directories, insurance atlases, transportation records, some electoral records, and some records of clubs, schools, and churches — will be in the Legislative Library, the Provincial Archives, the Rural Archives of Brandon University, in some public libraries, and in private or institutional collections, as was noted earlier. An introduction to these sources is provided by the booklet edited by P.H. Wichern, *Studies in Winnipeg Politics.*

CHAPTER 14

Writing a Book on Local History in Manitoba

If you are tireless, very interested, and determined, you may have noted all that has been said in the preceding pages but have wavered not at all in your purpose: to write a local history of the district. Good. How do you begin? With a central committee — a small group of people, perhaps five or seven, who share your enthusiasm, energy, and perseverance. They will be the heart of the project as well as its brain and muscle, so divide their tasks carefully. The largest job in terms of time and desk-work will be research and writing: three or four people should be committed to that assignment immediately. The other three posts will demand time and effort aplenty but in shorter bursts. These last three jobs require, too, special skills: a finance chairperson will manage the accounts and raise money to cover publication costs; a distribution chairperson will manage publicity, sales, and negotiations with bookstores; and an editor will supervise the final details associated with publication, such as the collection of maps and photographs, editing of captions, preparation of an index, supervision of proofreading, registration of copyright, and application for a standard book number. Four committees, therefore, would be ideal, but one or two people could, in a pinch, handle the last three jobs.

Research and writing will be long and arduous. Many local history groups find that it takes two or three years before a completed text is ready for the printer. The research group, which will immediately enlist the aid of four or five others, should ideally seek members who have had some history training. It might also be useful for some of its participants to enroll in university extension courses in regional or local history. The research and writing committee should have clear direction from the central committee on the nature of the work. The ideas and guidance in the preceding chapters should encourage you to aim higher than the typical product of yesterday —

capsule family histories plus short notes on institutions and businesses and clubs — and to attempt to interpret accurately the history of your district to outsiders. The simplest approach is to organize the book by chronological periods, as was suggested in the teachers' course outline (see p. 14). This will encourage you to think of your district as a community which experienced a series of changes over time as a result of the influences of personality, transportation systems, government and so on. Once these guidelines are clear, and the research committee is certain of its goal, it can set to work. Hold regular meetings, keep minutes, set time limits for discussion, and have a purpose or even an agenda for each meeting. Set up a home base for the project where books and notes and materials can be stored: a library or a school office might be ideal. Purchase supplies as they are needed: at the beginning, you will require plain paper (8 1/2 x 11 is standard), envelopes, file folders, and anything from cardboard boxes to file cabinets for storage. Finally, get the members to agree that they will work a specified time per week, perhaps a minimum of two hours, and encourage them to keep to a schedule. Many people have found that by setting aside one period on a certain evening or weekend, their task became something to look forward to rather than a reproachful shadow that never seemed to disappear.

Collect the essential secondary works, like Morton's history of Manitoba, and make sure that everyone has a chance to read them. Find out whether earlier works on your area are still available (see *Local History in Manitoba* and the other bibliographies), and obtain copies of all relevant material. Maintain a master bibliography, one card for each work you consult, in a separate file. Establish the important themes, events, and institutions in the district and, using the foregoing pages as a guide, set to work collecting research notes on them. Each time you work with a new source, place the bibliographic information on a card and file it in a separate bibliography file. Use half-sheets of 8-1/2" x 11" paper (this is cheaper than file cards), one side only, identify the source on each card (if only in abbreviated form), and then take notes which summarize or, if appropriate, quote your source. Place a title at the top of each card so that its content can be determined easily and quickly.

Because there will be many printed works that have a bearing on your community, it is wise to seek the assistance of a reference librarian at an early stage of your work. The librarian can introduce you to the standard bibliographies, and to the vast collections of government documents which defy easy organization. Included in this last group will be continuing series, such as the weather reports for your area, and items which may appear in the debates of the Legislature, the House of Commons, and the Senate, and in the journals and sessional papers of these bodies. You may require a librarian to show you the index to each volume and how to use it.

Another introductory step in research is to become familiar with the institutions that exist to serve you. Of all the libraries and archives in this category, the most important are the Provincial Archives of Manitoba, the Legislative Library of Manitoba, the Rural Archives of Brandon University, the three university libraries, and your local public library. The Legislative Library, located at 200 Vaughan Street, Winnipeg, contains a large number of books and government documents concerning Manitoba, the best collection of local histories in the province, the largest collection of Manitoba newspapers and journals anywhere, and most of the directories and other published sources mentioned in previous pages. The Provincial Archives, which is responsible for the preservation of documents and other materials related to the history of the province, devotes thousands of feet of shelf and file space to maps, photographs, government records and manuscript collections (such as letters and diaries and minute books and parish records). Both the library and the archives provide study space and copying facilities for researchers and, because of their attractive surroundings and helpful staff, are most congenial places of work. Letters to the Provincial Archivist and Provincial Librarian in advance of your first visit describing the topic of your research, the time at your disposal, and the goal of your project will enable the staff to prepare materials before you arrive. With advance warning, too, they will be able to introduce you to such helpful shortcuts as the vertical file on localities and families, the index to baptisms, and the biographical scrapbooks.

Several societies will be interested in your work and may be able to provide assistance and advice at various stages of the project. A list of these associations and their special areas of interest can be found in Appendix 5.

Historical resources outside the province may seem remote from the local study group but this need not be the case. There are two easy and convenient ways to discover whether important records related to your area have been preserved in national collections. First, consult a publication entitled *Union List of Manuscripts in Canadian Repositories/Catalogue collectif des manuscrits des archives canadiennes* (2 volumes, 2nd edition, 1977 with supplements), which is available in the Provincial Archives and many larger libraries. Check this list to find the libraries and archives that have information on your town and district, prominent citizens, ethnic groups, associations, unions and companies, and write the relevant archives to enquire about their particular collections. Second, if you are planning an extensive research project (one that will result in the publication of a full-scale history of town or district), write to the Public Archives of Canada, 395

Wellington Street, Ottawa, K1A 0N3, explaining your plans and asking for the assistance of its staff. If you have already consulted the published guides to portions of their collections (guides to groups of records in the Manuscript Collection, Public Records Collection and National Map Collection have been mentioned earlier and are available at the Provincial Archives of Manitoba), explain what you have seen and which sections of the papers might contain items of interest. If you wish one particular item, a map of your town in a certain year, for example, give its reference number and ask for the cost of duplication. The PAC duplicates most items at a reasonable price. Parts of its collection, too, are available on loan in microfilm form while some other important documentary sources, such as the papers of Sir John A. Macdonald, have been microfilmed and placed in the Provincial Archives. A list of other relevant archives is included in appendix 5.

If you plan to collect family histories, establish a master list with addresses of all former and current residents and send each a standard mimeographed questionnaire.

A day will come when you have seen not only many sources — that, you will learn, happens within a month or two — but more sources than you ever wanted to see, perhaps more than this book suggests, and certainly more than enough. When that moment arrives, perhaps two years after you begin, stop and take stock. The next phase is even tougher. A group of writers, preferably local talents who have been part of the research team, will now begin to work. What patterns are there in this mass of maps, photos, notes and tables? What is your district's story? To find out, this group must read the research collection and understand its contents thoroughly. They must establish chronological sections which explain the spirit and the changes in the district to outsiders who know nothing of rural Manitoba. The model proposed in chapter 1 may help:

1. Environment
2. Native-European contact in the fur trade era (to 1870 or 1880)
3. Transition to Canadian dominance and an agricultural economy, 1870s and 1880s
4. Town and district society in Manitoba's first generation, 1880s-1914
5. War and Social Change, 1914-30
6. Depression and War, 1930-46
7. The New Rural Society, 1946-

If this is helpful, use it; if you find or create a better model, by all means work with it.

A very helpful guide to preparing your manuscript and dealing with printers is *Into Print*, a paperback by Mary Hill and Wendall Cochran.

When the manuscript is completed, and a clean copy has been typed, the writers will heave a huge sigh of relief and think the job has finally been done. Their relief is understandable but they will be wrong. Now the importance of the other committees will become apparent. Let us deal with them as three separate groups.

The editorial committee will see the book from manuscript to publication. It may sound simple, but it requires patience, attention to detail, and considerable time. One major task of this group is to prepare material to supplement the written text. Pictures must be collected, given captions, and made ready for the printing process; a table of contents must be prepared; an introductory note or preface may be required; a list of maps and photos will be needed; and an index must be created. When this copy has gone to the printers, it will be typeset and proofs of the text will be returned for corrections. Mistakes made by the printer, and there are usually quite a few small errors, will be corrected free of charge; but you must pay for correction of mistakes that you have made. When the galleys are returned for final printing, you may also apply for the International Standard Book Number (ISBN) and register copyright. Your printer can advise you on these procedures.

The finance committee will have been visiting printers to determine costs of publication and, when the appearance of the manuscript is more or less final (length, illustrations, colour), will invite estimates or tenders. A 350 page hard-cover illustrated book could cost $10,000 to $20,000 or more, so these are important decisions. The finance committee will also have estimated the sales potential of the volume in order to determine the number of copies to be ordered. Manitobans have customarily printed between 1000 and 2000 copies in recent years but, because so much money is involved, the estimate should be prepared carefully. To an honest estimate of sales to former and present residents of the district, add no more than two to three hundred copies for general sales. The number of copies, the appearance of the book (paper quality, binding), the length of the manuscript, the number of illustrations, and the use of colour, will determine the printer's costs.

The next step will be an estimate of the volume price. The largest item here will be the printing costs, but you should also include the cost of stationery and research supplies, and the cost of either postage or a retail mark-up of at least 35 per cent. If you would like to have your book reviewed in newspapers and sold in several bookstores (those in the larger cities that specialize in Manitoba collections will often accept two or three copies on consignment), you must allow for the cost of distributing free review copies and for the minimum bookstore mark-up of 40 per cent. This mark-up can be partially avoided if you establish a lower pre-publication price (available to those who order and pay for the book prior to printing), but it must be maintained after publication if you are to retain the goodwill of booksellers. They are not interested in displaying your book if you charge two dollars less than they do.

The financial situation may dismay the local accountant. He will see for example, a $10,000 printing bill, 1000 volumes and 600 local buyers. Even if the book is priced at $14.00 and sold direct, the certain revenue (600 x $14 = $8400) will not make ends meet, let alone cover the research costs ($500), and postage (perhaps $750). And the accountant is likely to tell you that your inventory of 400 books is worth very little. More revenue must be obtained. Part of this task will fall on the distribution committee, whose duties are discussed below, but the finance committee can also seek grants to defray publication expenses. Local councils and businesses may wish to donate money; do not hesitate to raise the matter. If you are establishing an extensive collection of local documents, the school board might purchase it after the writing is completed. Explain to the board members that local archives are valuable educational aids (see chapter 1). Provincial government grants are often difficult to secure, but the Historic Resources Branch, Department of Cultural Affairs and Historical Resources, can advise you on these possibilities. The federal Department of the Secretary of State maintains a branch office in Winnipeg where, again, advice is available on federal grants. Do not rely on the two senior levels of government, however, because neither is likely to find the money when you need it. If you are within one or two thousand dollars of your budget, and have inventory to cover this amount, try a local bank or credit union. And do push your distributors to sell more books.

The distribution committee will begin its work when the project begins. It must ensure that the book is purchased, so publicity must be secured every step of the way. When the project is announced, letters should go to all the local and farm newspapers asking for space to publicize the venture. In these announcements, ask, too, whether readers have pictures or documents relating to your district. With the subscription list of the local newspapers as a base (your relationship with editor and publisher is obviously important), compile an address list of potential buyers. (This will also serve as an aid in the finance committee's work). Next, write letters to the editors of newspapers in other parts of the continent where former district residents might now live, requesting assistance with the project. These are often printed free-of-charge in the "Letters to the Editor" column. When the book is ready to launch, mail a publicity brochure with return envelopes if possible, to every potential buyer, requesting orders and payments. On the publication day, hold a party, perhaps in conjunction with a major district event such as a sports day, dance, or homecoming, to announce your achievement. In some towns, the first copies off the press are numbered by hand, certified by the printer, and auctioned to help defray expenses. Put the books in appropriate stores and then (not before) mail review copies to journals which are important in your district. This group might include local papers, the farm and co-operative newspapers, and radio and television stations in the area. Send copies to the Manitoba Historical Society, for the McWilliams award competition, and to the Canadian Historical Association for consideration in the Regional History Committee Award of Merit competition. Finally, keep in touch with the bookstores carrying your volume in order that they remain aware of its importance and keep the book in stock.

Remember, finally, that the book was begun for good reasons. Take your time: even three or four years is not unusual for the completion of a local history. The result will be an achievement you and others will always treasure.

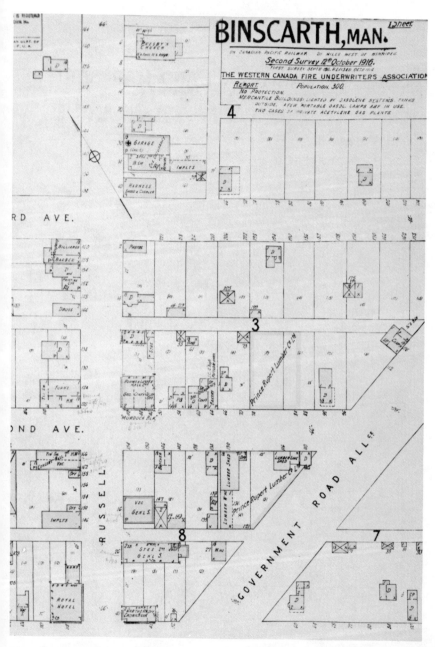

Part of Binscarth, Manitoba, 1916 (courtesy Public Archives of Manitoba)

From "Cummins Manitoba Land Map Series", about 1918 (courtesy Public Archives of Manitoba)

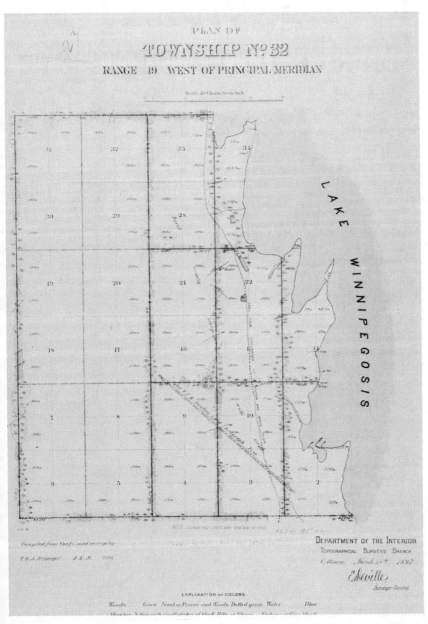

Plan of Township No. 32, 1897 (courtesy Public Archives of Manitoba)

MANITOBA
MUNICIPALITIES DIRECTORY.

NOTE.—The names in this section of the Directory should be read as follows : Abbott Henry, 24, 18, 27, Elphinstone, the figures stand for Section 24, Township 18, Range 27, the Post Office, Elphinstone.

A'Bear Edmund, lab., Stonewall
Abbey Hy. carpenter, 23, 24, 41, Carberry
" Moses, 12, 4, 6, Melita.
Abey John. Douglas
" M. G., 22, 11, 18, Chater.
" Thos., 5, 11, 7, Douglas.
Abbott. A. E., 7, 7, 15, Stockton
" Benj., 3, 3, 24, Deloraine.
" Chas. 15, 3, 27, Melita.
" Henry, 24, 18, 17, Elphinstone
" **Hugh, lot 33, Emerson**
" Jas., 24, 18, 27, Elphinstone
" J. J., photographer, Emerson
" J. S., 7, 7, 15, Stockton
" **Robt., lab., Stonewall**
" **Thos., 10, 8, 21, Souris**
" Wm., agent, Stockton
" **Wm., guard, Stony Mountain**
" Wm., 32, 15, 18, Minnedosa.
Abel Alex., 28, 15, 18, Minnedosa
" **E. R., Selkirk**
" Peter, 32, 14, 18, Clanwilliam
Abery Jer., 30, 7, 22, Souris
Abey Chas., 36, 10, 19, Chater
" John. 5, 11, 17, Chater
Abby Levi, 13, 10, 15, Carberry
Abraham
" Johann, 15, 2, 1, Gretna
" James, 5, 8, 10, Holland
" Joseph, 31, 7, 23, Deleau
" O., 14, 7, 24, Delean.
Abrahamson
" Fred., 24, 7, 29, Reston
" Johan, 28, 6, 29, Sinclair.
" Johann, 6, 19, 4 , Gimli
" Jon, 30, 6, 29, Sinclair.
" Jno., 16, 8, 4, Gimli
" Kris., 20, 6, 29, Sinclair.
Abrams Heinrich, 7, 1, 1, Gretna
" Jacob, 8, 1, 1, Gretna
" Johann, jun., 10, 12, 1, Gretna
" Johann, 8, 1, 1, Gretna
" Johann, 10, 2, 1, Gretna
" Peter, sen., 4, 1, 1, Gretna
" Peter, jun, 4, 1, 1, Gretna
" **Samuel, Mid'le Church**
Absalom Geo. W., 32, 16, 25, Warleigh
" George, engineer, Birtle
Acar Louis S. M., 36, 17, 13, Tuppert

Acaster
" Herbert, livery, Methven.
" H., 18, 2, 18, Lyonshalt
" Wm., 21, 2, 18, Wakora
Acheson Alex., St. Charles
" John, sen., 28, 9, 27, Virden.
" Joseph, 25, 12, 9, Burnside
" Herbert, 4, 8, 21, Souris
" R., 28, 1, 7, Thornhill
Ackerman Albert, 10, 11, 6, P La Prairie
" **Geo.. 10, 11, 6, Portage la Prairie**
Ackroyd James, 7, 5, 22, West Hall.
Acres J. H., 21, 2, 3, Dominion City
" W. S., 21, 2, 3, Dominion City
Acton John, 32, 3, 17, Killarney
" Arthur, clerk, Brandon.
" W. H., 30, 9, 21, Alexander
Adair Thos., 13, 8, 9, Treherne
" **James, 23, 8, 9, Rathwell**
" John, Treherne.
" J. W. Portage La Prairie.
" **S., 32, 14, 13, Arden**
" S., carpenter, Portage La Prairie.
" Thomas, 12, 8, 9, Rathwell
" **Wm., 36, 10, 6e, Millbrook**
" Wm., 19, 11, 29, Elkhorn
Adam
" James, 2, 6, 29, Sinclair.
" James, 24, 6, 21, Fairfax.
" John, lab., lot 13, Baie St. Paul
" Wlfd., merchant, 4, 25, 19, Gartmore
Adams Alf., Portage La Prairie
" Abraham, 25, 3, 24, Bo'ssevain.
" Alex., 7, 7, 7, Clearsprings
" Chas., merchant. Brandon
" Cyrus, engineer, Birtle.
" Frank, 2, 14, 2, Woodlands
" Geo., 28, 10, 20, Kemnay.
" Geo., Portage La Prairie
" **Geo. Rev., St. Boniface**
" **H., hotel, Portage La Prairie**
" H., 25, 6, 13, Cypress River
" **James, 21, 12, 6, Portage la Prairie**
" James, laborer, 9, 11, 11, Austin
" James W., 21, 12, 6, High Bluff
" James, laborer, Brandon.
" John, 26, 5, 20, Heaslip.
" John, 9, 3, 12, Clearwater
" John, 7, 12, 6, Cook's Creek

Henderson's Manitoba and N.W.T. Gazetteer and Directory, 1898 (courtesy Public Archives of Manitoba)

BAPTISMS.

Municipality of _Gimli_   Congregation of _Mikley (Hecla Man)_

	No. **1**	No.	No. **2**
When born.	Jan. 16th., 1901		May 28th., 1901
Where born	Hecla, Man.		Hecla, Man.
Name.	Kristjin Felix		Thorunn Lara
Sex—Male or Female.	M.		F.
Name and Surname of Father.	Siggie Sigurdsson		Vilhjálmur Sigurgeirsson's
Name and Maiden Surname of Mother.	Sigurveig Jónsdóttir		Kristin Helgadóttir —
Occupation or Calling of Father.	Farmer		Farmer
Signature, Description and Residence of Informant.	S. Sigurdsson, the childs father. Hecla, Man.		V. Sigurgeirsson, childs father, Hecla, Man
When Baptized. Signature of Clergyman or Minister.	Ap. 20th., 1901 P. Martinsson.		Dec. 29th., 1901 R. Martinsson
REMARKS.			

	No. **3**	No. **4**	No. **5**
When born.	June 20th, 1901.	March 12th, 1902	Nov. 3rd., 1901.
Where born	Big Island	Big Island	Big Island
Name.	Steingrimur Halldór	Helgi Kristinn	Brynjólfur Aladdin
Sex—Male or Female.	M.	M.	M.
Name and Surname of Father.	Jón Sigurgeirsson	Eggert Thordarson	Marin J. Doll
Name and Maiden Surname of Mother.	Sigurlina Hall-dórsdóttir	Kristin Hallfríður Ásbjörnsdóttir	Helga Ingibjörg Brynjólfs-dóttir
Occupation or Calling of Father.	Fisherman	Fisherman	Fisherman
Signature, Description and Residence of Informant.	Mrs. Sigurgeirsson, childs mother, Hecla, Man.	E. Thordarson, childs father, Hecla, Man.	M. J. Doll, childs father, Hecla, Man.
When Baptized. Signature of Clergyman or Minister.	June 15th., 1901 Brynjólfur Martinsson	March 17th., 1902. N. S. Thorlaksson	June 14th., 1902. R. Martinsson
REMARKS.			

Hecla Lutheran Church Baptismal Record, 1901 (courtesy Public Archives of Manitoba)

TABLE **IV**—Birth Places of the People.

DISTRICTS.	SUB-DISTRICTS. — SOUS-DISTRICTS.	British Isles. — Iles Britanniques.			Canada.			
		England and Wales. — Angleterre et Galles.	Ireland. — Irlande.	Scotland. — Ecosse.	Prince Edward Island. — Ile du Prince-Edouard	Nova Scotia. — Nouvelle-Ecosse.	New Brunswick. — Nouv.-Brunswick.	Quebec. — Québec.
	a. Rhineland	6	2	1	......	......	......	......
	b. Dufferin, *South—Sud.*	243	67	138	5	30	4	82
	c. Carleton	106	54	102	......	7	......	60
	d. Dufferin, *North—Nord*	68	41	93	12	5	2	45
	e. Douglas	17	3	6	......	4	......	3
	f. Louise	181	57	88	1	6	1	53
	g. Derby	123	67	48	1	10	......	8
	h. Argyle	95	35	56	16	14	4	47
	i. Lorne	109	53	43	1	22	5	353
	j. Oakland	116	32	78	......	48	......	1
	k. Glenwood	100	85	39	2	14	4	5
	l. Whitehead	170	33	55	4	28	7	39
	m. Cornwallis	144	46	98	2	43	14	50
	n. Elton	130	63	54	......	46	2	34
	o. Daly	181	12	81	......	3	6	7
1. Selkirk	*p.* Turtle Mountain	106	22	80	2	3	7	82
	q. Deloraine	112	27	74	......	10	1	23
	r. Whitewater	87	54	62	1	4	1	23
	s. Riverside	104	28	49	7	13	4	39
	t. Medora	67	18	18	......	20	8	2
	u. Arthur	58	21	23	......	11	7	19
	v. Inchiquin	12	1	10	......	......	......	5
	w. Brenda	20	7	20	......	12	......	12
	x. Sifton	84	12	35	......	11	4	93
	y. Pipestone	77	16	62	......	3	1	8
	z. Wallace	263	60	160	......	26	38	41
	aa. Woodworth	76	34	49	......	26	......	53
	bb. Brandon, *City—Ville.*	315	68	149	3	84	67	91
	cc. Nelson, *Town—Ville.*	5	10	3	1	5	1	......
	dd. Pilot Mound, *Town-V.*	7	......	6	......	......	1	......
	Total	3,182	1,028	1,780	58	508	189	1,283
	a. Elm River	38	3	10	......	3	......	13
	b. Portage la Prairie	155	100	153	2	37	6	28
	c. Norfolk, *South—Sud*	151	53	70	1	19	1	23
	d. Norfolk, *North—Nord*	126	43	92	......	......	......	46
	e. Cypress, *South—Su t.*	134	23	56	......	8	8	49
	f. Cypress, *North—Nord*	88	47	94	......	10	3	16
	g. Westbourne	71	49	78	4	24	4	22
	h. Osprey	5	9	32	......	1	......	......
	i. Glendale	63	35	17	3	2	......	7
	j. Lansdowne	67	19	65	2	1	......	5
	k. Rosedale	44	32	25	......	......	......	5
	l. Riding Mountain	9	......	......	......	......	......	......
	m. Odanah	89	20	86	......	4	3	6

Census of 1886, Province of Manitoba, Table IV: Birthplace (courtesy Public Archives of Manitoba)

TABLEAU **IV**—Population par lieux de Naissance.

Canada.				Other B'sh Poss'ns. Autres poss'ns Brit.			Fran- ce.	Ger ma- l. y.	Ice- land.	Ita- ly.	Rus- sia and Po- land.	Swe- den, N. and Den- mark.	Uni- ted States	Other Coun- tries.	At Sea.	Not gi- ven.
On- tario.	Mani- toba.	B'sh Co- lum bia. Co- lom bie- Brit	The Terri- tories Les Terri toires.	New- found land. Terre- neuve	Chan- nel Is- land. Iles de la Man- che.	Other Pos- ses- sions. Autres Pos- ses- sions.	Fran- ce.	Alle ma- gne	Is- lande.	Ita- lie.	Rus- sie et Polo- gne.	Suède Nor- vège, Dane- mark.	Etats- Unis.	Autres con- trées	En mer	Non don nés.
27	1,505	....	......	......	......	......	......	2	8	......	2,409	......	4	......	......	......
1,225	538	....	1	......	......	2	1	20	2	......	85	15	71	2	......	4
347	199	..	......	..	1	......	......	1	......	......	......	......	1	......	......	......
724	339	....	2	1	......	1	1	2	......	....	......	4	17	1	......	....
88	1,028	....	......	......	......	......	1	21	......	....	1,476	2	25	5	2	....
1,125	382	....	1	......	....	6	1	4	1	....	3	8	19	3	......	....
521	162	....	1	......	..	......	1	......	....	......	......	3	18	1	......	2
513	257	....	2	......	1	2	......	....	237	......	......	......	7	......	......	....
564	538	1	....	......	......	2	......	20	......	......	1	1	96	......	......	....
208	126	......	......	......	......	1	......	9	......	....	......	2	3	......	......	15
450	120	......	......	......	......	7	......	. .	......	......	......	......	9	......	......	...
415	118	......	1	5	......	2	......	10	......	......	......	3	25	2	......	....
486	129	1	......	2	... ...	......	......	2	......	..	......	......	23	8	1	....
484	187	......	......	......	......	5	......	8	......	....	......	2	4	......	......	....
227	113	......	......	......	......	4	......	3	......	......	......	......	7	......	......	...
412	130	. ...	3	1	......	2	....	......	......	......	......	2	38	4	......	.....
529	154	......	....	......	......	4	......	.. ...	......	......	......	4	18	5	......	1
638	103	......	......	......	......	3	1	1	......	......	......	......	18	1	......	....
477	93	......	......	......	......	1	......	....	......	......	......	......	8	......	......	....
519	88	......	......	......	......	.....	......	6	......	......	1	......	4	......	......	6
246	48	......	1	......	......	1	......	......	......	......	......	......	6	......	......	7
47	12	......	......	......	......	......	......	... ..	......	......	......	....	......	......	......	12
231	41	... .	......	......	......	......	......	. 6	......	......	......	......	3	......	......	....
170	119	......	4	......	......	......	3	...	......	......	......	8	19	......	......	....
268	396	......	......	......	......	1	......	1	......	......	......	......	4	......	......	....
468	97	......	1	......	......	......	......	11	......	.	......	13	6	......	......	....
621	258	......	......	......	......	2	1	2	......	......	......	......	14	......	......	....
1,218	286	......	2	1	......	2	2	5	......	......	......	6	46	2	......	1
23	24	......	......	......	......	......	......	......	......	......	......	1	......	......	......	....
21	18	......	1	......	......	......	......	......	......	......	......	......	......	......	......	......
13,592	7,613	2	19	11	2	48	11	135	248	......	3,975	74	513	34	3	48
50	225	......	4	....	......	... ..	1	1	......	....	......	1	4	......	......	3
1,204	1,173	1	29	......	......	1	......	15	......	1	......	31	14	1	......	....
462	228	......	1	......	......	2	2	8	25	......	1	7	25	1	...	....
242	111	......	......	......	......	1	......	6	3	......	10	30	1	......	......	5
380	114	......	......	......	......	1	4	1	......	......	1	12	......	......	1
915	296	......	......	......	......	1	......	6	......	... ..	7	8	.... ..	......	2
406	826	......	1	......	......	......	......	......	......	......	6	23	......	......	83
189	51	......	......	......	......	......	1	......	......	......	4	......	......	....
281	128	......	......	......	......	2	......	1	......	......	1	11	......	......	2
254	165	......	......	......	......	1	1	......	......	......	13	......	......	....
264	249	......	1	......	......	......	10	......	1	1	1	3	43	......	....
11	58	......	2	......	......	......	......	......	......	......	......	......	......	......	......
319	135	......	......	......	......	3	......	4	......	......	7	,8	7	......	....

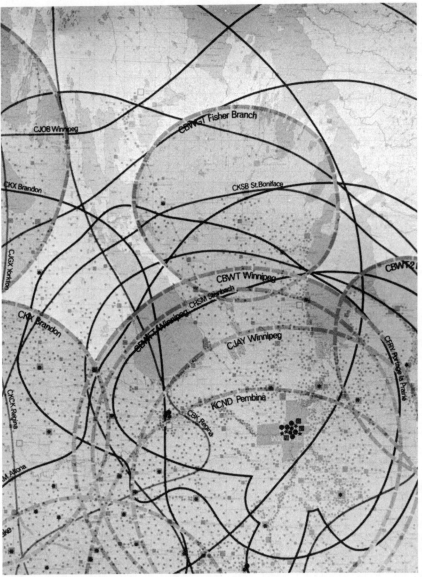

News Media Coverage, 1971 (taken from the Regional Analysis Program, Southern Manitoba, courtesy Manitoba Department of Industry and Commerce)

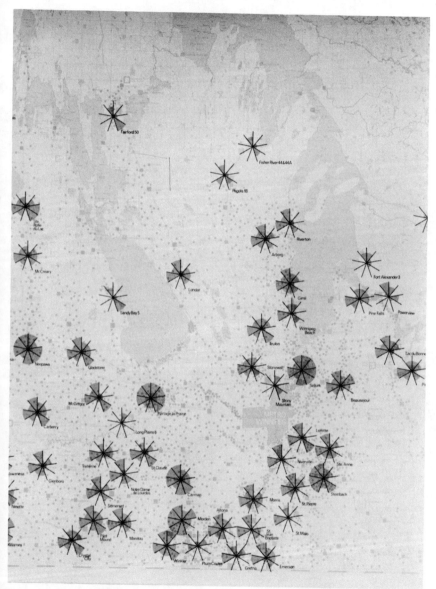

Infrastructure: Levels of service to urban settlements and Indian bands with a population over 500, 1971 (taken from the Regional Analysis Program, Southern Manitoba, courtesy Manitoba Department of Industry and Commerce)

An Introduction to the Study of Land and Settlement Records

D.M. LOVERIDGE

Land and settlement records can provide a different perspective on local history and agriculture. The factors involved in the settlement of a district — an individual's financial standing, his perceptions of soil and landscape, the quality, quantity and price of available land, and the policies of government and private land agencies — all can be studied in these records. Many local historians have recognized the importance of such sources, but they have often used them merely to compile a list of the first owners of quarter-sections. Such lists are usually inaccurate and are rarely used to interpret the course of local development. The local experience must be measured against the practice of land distribution in the province, and this interpretation must be based on a knowledge both of federal policies and local land ownership records.

The first agricultural settlers in the area now known as Manitoba were located along the lower Red and Assiniboine rivers in several small communities. In the early part of the nineteenth century, the river frontages were surveyed into "river lots" similar to those used in Quebec. These consisted of parallel strips which were usually ten chains (660 feet) on the river front and two miles deep with a further two miles of "hay privilege" land added. By 1869 this survey system had been extended along the Red River from Pembina to Lower Fort Garry, and along the Assiniboine from its junction with the Red west to Portage la Prairie. As the Canadian takeover of the settlement drew near in 1869, Ontario surveyors were sent to resurvey these lots. Some local inhabitants interpreted this work as a preliminary step in cheating them out of their lands, for Hudson's Bay Company land titles

* A glossary of terms used in the study of land and settlement records can be found at the end of this appendix.

were not always clear. The new survey was thus one of the factors which incited the insurrection of 1869-70. In the end, when Manitoba became a Canadian province in 1870, existing titles were guaranteed and the river lot system was left intact; however, the lots were renumbered to fit into the new survey and title systems.

Manitoba, like Saskatchewan and Alberta, and unlike the other seven provinces in the Dominion, was created by the federal government from federally owned territories rather than changed in status from British colony to Canadian province. Because western settlement was crucial to the future development of the new Dominion, and because there were few vested interests to object, all ungranted lands (those not on the rivers) in Manitoba and the North-West Territories, as Saskatchewan and Alberta were then called, were held under federal control "for the purposes of the Dominion." Control of the remaining ungranted lands was not transferred to the three prairie provinces until 1930.

Before it could actually make use of its new western property, the Dominion had to survey its holdings and subdivide them into smaller and more manageable units. After some consideration, a uniform "sectional survey system" covering the whole of the West was adopted. With a few minor exceptions,* this survey divided all land south and west of the Canadian Shield into six-mile-square "townships." Each township consisted of 36 one-mile-square "sections," which were further divided into four 160-acre "quarter-sections." The quarter-section could then be divided into four 40-acre "legal subdivisions" (*L.S.*) or "lots." In cities, towns and villages, and where otherwise needed, the *L.S.* could be divided yet again into "blocks."

Locating any piece of land in southern and northwestern Manitoba is very simple. Each township has a township number and a range number (such as 7-23). The first number describes its position in a horizontal row of townships north of the 49th parallel. For example, the southern edge of any township in township row 7 is exactly 36 miles north of the international boundary, and its northern edge 42 miles north. The range number gives its position in a vertical column of townships in relation to a given north-south "meridian" line. All Manitoba ranges are numbered by their position east or west of the "Principal Meridian," which is located just west of Winnipeg. The Rural Municipality of Sifton, for example, consists of nine townships arranged in a square. All of these lie in three range-columns (23, 24, 25), all of which are west of the Principal Meridian (W1). The eastern edge of any

---

* These exceptions include the linear river lot survey of pre-1870 vintage, on the Red and lower Assiniboine rivers, and some areas adjacent to meridian and correction lines, where the cumulative error of the survey resulted in odd-sized or partial townships.

township in range 23 W1 is exactly 132 miles west of the meridian, and its western edge is 138 miles west. Any given township in Manitoba can therefore be identified by stating the number of its township row (e.g., 7) and of its range column (e.g., 23). The resulting co-ordinate (e.g. 7-23 W1) can identify only one township, and its physical location can readily be determined.

The 36 one-mile-square sections within each township are numbered transversely from east to west, working up the grid. Thus section 1 is in the southeast corner and section 6 is in the southwest corner. Section 7 is above 6, and section 12 above 1, and so on; ending up with section 36 in the northeast corner (see Figure 1). Each section is divided into four 160-acre quarters, which are identified by compass directions: northwest, northeast, southwest, and southeast (see Figure 2). Each quarter-section is further divided into four 40-acre legal subdivisions (L.S.). These are numbered on a sectional basis, in the same fashion as sections in a township (see Figure 3).

Using this system it is possible to state the location of any point in the surveyed area of Manitoba (and western Canada) both concisely and with great precision. To give one example, the archaeological excavations recently conducted on the north shore of Oak Lake (west of Brandon) were in the northwest corner of legal subdivision 13, the northwest lot of the southwest quarter-section of section 31 in township 8 of range 24, west of the Principal Meridian. Or more conveniently, NW L.S. 13 SW 31-8-21 W1.

31	32	33	34	35	36
30	29	28	27	26	25
19	20	21	22	23	24
18	17	16	15	14	13
7	8	9	10	11	12
6	5	4	3	2	1

NW	NE
SW	SE

13	14	15	16
12	11	10	9
5	6	7	8
4	3	2	1

FIGURE 1: Sections in township

FIGURE 2: Quarters in section

FIGURE 3: Legal sub-divisions in section

Between the sections, strips of land were reserved for the construction of roads. These are known as "road allowances." In southern Manitoba, under the "First System" of survey, these consisted of a 99-foot (1-1/2 chains) right-of-way, with a total of 72 miles of road allowance in each township. North of Duck Mountain, under the "Third System," only half of the east-west strips were reserved. Together with all of the north-south lines, this made a total of only 54 miles per township. In addition, the allowances were narrower, only 66 feet wide (1 chain). The survey work in the province was begun in 1869-70 and was basically completed by the mid-1880s.

The uniformity of the sectional survey system is a great advantage in historical research on the prairies. With a good map, and a modest amount of practice, it can easily be learned. It is particularly important to understand the mechanics of the numerical location system because virtually all records of land description, ownership and disposal employ it as the basis of their arrangement.

Generally speaking, Dominion lands in Manitoba were assigned to one of three categories of disposition and disposal by the government. A large part was set aside to compensate different corporations for their contribution to the development of the West. These included the Hudson's Bay Company and the various railway companies. Other lands, a small proportion, were reserved for specific governmental purposes, such as the endowment for schools and compensation to the Manitoba provincial government. The last category and the largest one, consisted of Dominion lands intended for rapid transfer into the hands of settlers by means of free homesteads, low-priced pre-emptions, and ordinary sales.

Privately owned corporations received a considerable proportion of the Dominion lands in Manitoba. The Hudson's Bay Company, for example, received approximately two sections in every township in the West in return for surrendering its title to the area in 1869. Many railway companies received land subsidies from the Dominion to assist in their construction of rail lines. The most important of these grants went to the Canadian Pacific Railway Company, which in 1881 received $25 million and 25 million acres of land to build the first transcontinental railway. It later received more land for the construction of branch lines. Many others also received subsidies, such as the Winnipeg Great Northern, and the Lake Manitoba Railway and Canal Co., the Manitoba and South Eastern, the Manitoba and North Western, and the Manitoba and South-Western Colonization Railway Co. Various "colonization companies" also received Dominion land grants for bringing settlers to specific areas. Some of these corporate grants took the form of reduced prices on Dominion lands, but most were outright grants. The corporations were expected to sell their grant lands to settlers in order to recover expenses.

After 1881, corporate grants were usually limited to specific sections within townships. The H.B.C. received section 8 and all or part of section 26 in every township, except where settlers had "squatted" on those sections before survey. Railway grant lands were usually restricted to the odd-numbered sections (1, 3, 5, etc.) in a township, except sections 11 and 29 which were the school lands. In contrast to the American pattern, where railway companies received grants along the line under construction, the Canadian land grant policy usually stated that subsidy lands must be "fairly fit for settlement." This often meant that railway companies, particularly the CPR went far afield to find suitable lands. (In 1894, for example, in return for building its Pipestone Branch in Southwestern Manitoba, the CPR reserved lands in central Saskatchewan.) As a result, most areas of Manitoba, regardless of their distance from subsidized lines, had reserved railway lands.

The most important of the federal reserved lands were those set aside for educational purposes. This land, usually sections 11 and 29 of every township, was to be sold at the highest possible price and the profit was to be used to support education. Much of the land was not sold until late in the settlement period.

The Dominion also assigned lands to the province of Manitoba to compensate it for the fact that the Dominion owned all of the land in the province after the transfer from the HBC in 1869-70. In 1885, two different grants were made. The University of Manitoba received 150,000 acres to sell for its support (thus theoretically relieving the province of the cost of maintaining the university). More directly the province was also given all Dominion lands classified as Swamp (or marsh), which were to be sold to supplement provincial revenue. Most of these provincial lands were not actually selected until the early 1890s, and could not be sold until the second land boom of the early 1900s. The unsold balance of the Swamp Lands was given back to the Dominion in 1912 in return for a cash subsidy. Much of the Swamp Land grant was in the Interlake region, while most of the Manitoba University Grant (70 percent) was in western Manitoba.

The balance of the Dominion lands remaining after the above-mentioned grants had been made were used to promote settlement. While the 160-acre "free" homestead is the best known example of the federal land policy, inexpensive pre-emption and ordinary sales and other forms of transfer also played a part. The relative importance of these different means of transferring lands to settlers varied considerably over time.

In 1872 the first Dominion Lands Act (35 Vic. c.23) was passed. This act enabled anyone who was over twenty-one or was the head of a family to settle on a 160-acre homestead, and eventually obtain title to the land. The homestead was not entirely free, for the settler had to pay a $10 fee to register and had to fulfil rather strict conditions of living on and cultivating the land to gain ownership of it, but it was, even with these provisions, an inexpensive way to settle. In 1874 it was further decided that homesteaders could also make an "interim entry" on a vacant, adjacent quarter-section. This meant that the land would be reserved until the settlers had gained title to their homesteads, when they could decide whether to buy the "pre-emption." These provisions sounded very generous, but in fact they were misleading. Until 1881 most Dominion lands within five or ten miles of a railway route had to be purchased; and access to the railway was vital to a settler. As long as the Dominion government planned to build the Pacific railway itself, it could not afford to give away the closest and most valuable lands whose sale would pay for the line.

This state of affairs was altered suddenly in 1881 when the construction of a transcontinental railway became the task of the CPR, a private syndicate. Relieved of this burden, the Dominion government was able to "give away" its lands, regardless of their location. At least half of the land — that on even-numbered sections, less the HBC's sections 8 and 26 — in any area was available. Homestead regulations were accordingly loosened in the 1880s, making it relatively easy for almost anyone to acquire a 160-acre homestead and a 160 acre pre-emption. While the rules were tightened somewhat at the end of the decade, by then the greater part of southern Manitoba had been settled.

The majority of settlers acquired a homestead from the Dominion, fulfilling the set conditions. Many then took up their low-priced pre-emption quarter. Some, however, purchased Dominion lands instead. A certain number of these used one form or other of "scrip" (certificates issued by the Dominion which could be exchanged for land). Scrip was issued by the government for several reasons, including compensation for Army and North-West Mounted Police veterans and, most importantly, as a grant to the new Manitoba Metis to ensure their unchallenged settlement according to the new laws of the land. The scrip was used in the same way as cash, and was often sold or exchanged by the original owners. Others bought Dominion lands outright. Such "ordinary sales" had no extra conditions attached. The price varied with the quality of the land and its distance from the railway, but was usually quite reasonable. In the early period at least, when a great deal of land was open, the size of a settler's holding was restricted only by the size of his pocketbook and imagination.

The cheapest and easiest way for settlers to acquire land was through a homestead and pre-emption, but some did not wish to be burdened with the various homestead conditions, and others found that Dominion land was not available where they wished to settle. In these cases settlers might purchase land in the various corporate reserves or, if it was then for sale, from the School or provincial grants. Generally speaking, these lands were more expensive than those sold by the Dominion; normally, the railway lands were the cheapest and the HBC and School lands the highest priced. This variation was largely due to different land disposal policies. Most of the railway companies, and especially the CPR, wished to increase railway traffic. To do this they had to encourage settlement, and to encourage settlement they had to offer their lands at relatively low prices. The HBC, however, had no other interest than to garner the highest possible price. Similarly, the School lands had (by law) to be sold at the best possible price, as determined by the judgement of the grant's trustees. Thus these lands were generally much higher priced than the railway lands. Possibly the most expensive lands were those held by the land companies. These organizations, like the HBC, were interested only in profits. Moreover, they were often speculators, buying land cheaply and selling only when the best possible price could be realized.

Not all of the Dominion lands homesteaded or sold either went into, or stayed in, the hands of actual settlers. Much land was acquired by speculators, individual and corporate. Whether seeking a quick profit or long-term gains, speculators often inhibited the process of settlement in an area by deliberately withholding good land from sale, or by pricing it beyond the means of most settlers. Simply by undertaking an agreement of sale or a homestead contract on a piece of land, and then not following through with payments or improvements, a speculator could keep it off the market and out of use. This was also the case where actual settlers, for one reason or another, failed to fulfil contract conditions. It might take some time for the Dominion or corporate owner to clarify the situation and cancel the contract, making the land available again. For any of these reasons, or a combination of them, the actual amount of vacant land in a given area which was available for settlement could be restricted.

In attempting to dispose of their lands, the Dominion, the corporations, and the province had one major problem in common: the high rate of failure among settlers. Establishing oneself as a farmer or rancher in the west was not an easy process, and many who moved onto the land did not succeed. As a result, pieces of land were often "sold" or "entered" on several occasions before finally passing into the hands of a permanent settler. On the whole, the higher the price of the land, the lower was the rate of cancellation of contracts; this rule does not apply, however, during the unstable "boom" of 1881-2 when free homestead and cheap sale lands also experienced a high turnover. Unfortunately, many of these failed transactions were not recorded, and thus it is hard to determine the rate or degree of failure in any given area. One special type of homestead that is of interest here is the "80-acre" homestead. This type of entry, consisting of an 80-acre homestead and an 80-acre pre-emption on the same quarter, was permitted in 1883-86. Since these entries were allowed only on previously cancelled homestead quarters, they give some indication of instances of failure in the early years. On the whole, however, success is more likely to be recorded in surviving documents than is failure.

The disposition of lands in many Manitoba townships followed a roughly similar pattern. The HBC and the School land grants occupied sections

8 and 26, and 11 and 29, respectively, while railway lands took up the remaining odd-numbered sections (except where the land was of a markedly low quality). The balance consisted of unreserved Dominion lands open to homestead, pre-emption and sale, though some of these might be allotted to the Manitoba University or Swamp land provincial grants. The disposition of lands in a "typical township" is shown in Figure 4.

R	D	R	D	R	D
D	S	D	R	H	R
R	D	R	D	R	D
D	R	D	R	D	R
R	H	R	D	S	D
D	R	D	R	D	R

R = railway
D = unreserved Dominion
S = School
H = HBC

FIGURE 4: Disposition of lands in a township

Students should be warned, however, that this is no more than a very general plan, and that there were many exceptions in any locality. The general plan is applicable primarily to areas settled after 1881 (which excludes most of southeastern Manitoba), and which lie in good areas near the original CPR main line or its earlier branches (which excludes most of northern, northwestern and eastern Manitoba). Further, in its main areas of applicability, great variations can be found at the local level where "squatters" (pre-survey settlers), terrain and other special circumstances often caused adjustments to be made.

SOURCES

The study of land ownership records is not easy, and there is no single source which provides all of the information required. Most researchers will probably be interested in the first settlers or, more generally, in the initial process of settlement in their area. (Who went where, when? How did they establish themselves?) But, whatever the exact aim of the project, certain basic preparations should be made before any land ownership research is attempted.

First, read several general histories of settlement. The Red River land system and its ownership records are a study in themselves. For a general description of the system, see W.L. Morton, *Manitoba: A History*, chaps. 3 and 4. The careful work of J.L. Tyman, *By Section, Township and Range*, will be very helpful. The best single introduction to the land records is Archer

Martin's *The Hudson's Bay Company Land Tenures and the Occupation of Assiniboia by Lord Selkirk's Settlers*, especially pp. 117-33. The Hudson's Bay Company Archives in Winnipeg has originals or copies of the main Red River land registers, including the copy of land Register B (E6/2) which is described in detail by Martin. Another useful reference is the *Correlation Book of Hudson's Bay Company and Dominion Government Survey Numbers.* This book, which is available in the Provincial Archives of Manitoba, Red River Collection, lists the old and new numbers of the river lots and is indispensable for tracing the old land records relating to modern lots. For a discussion of the "purposes of the Dominion," see Chester Martin, *"Dominion Lands" Policy.*

On land grants, see: J.S. Galbraith, "Land Policies of the Hudson's Bay Company," and Martin, *Dominion Lands,* for a discussion of the нвс grant; J.B. Hedges, *Building the Canadian West,* for the cpr grant; and the same author's *Federal Railway Subsidy Policy in Canada,* for railway grants generally. Tyman, *By Section, Township and Range,* discusses land grants to "colonization companies." Both Tyman (p. 190) and Martin, *"Dominion Lands,"* (p. 106) discuss the School lands, and Tyman describes the Manitoba University grant (pp. 198-99).

For summaries of homestead legislation, see Tyman (chaps. 3 and 4) and Martin (chap. 9). The same authors discuss scrip (Tyman, pp. 27-28, and Martin, pp. 21-22), and Tyman deals at length with speculation (chap. 15). You may also find it useful to consult local histories at this stage.

The second step is to acquire a good set of maps of the area. The best available are those in the National Topographic System. Several different scales are available, but historians will probably find the 250,000 and 50,000 scale the most useful. The former give an overview of a region at a scale of about four miles to the inch, while the latter are good for local details (about one mile to the inch). Both give township and range co-ordinates and outlines. These may be obtained from the Canada Map Office, Surveys and Mapping Branch, Department of Energy, Mines and Resources, 615 Booth Street, Ottawa, K1A 0E9. Topical maps featuring soils and various other characteristics are also available (see appendix 2 on agricultural capability ratings.) These various maps are both informative and inexpensive. An illustrated guide to their use, by L.M. Sebert, entitled *Every Square Inch: The Story of Canadian Topographic Mapping* is available from the same source for a nominal price.

Once you have a working knowledge of the potential of your area, and of the possible problems ahead, the next step is to decide *exactly* what area will be covered in the search. This may be a town, a township, a rural municipality, or a specific region. In any case, the exact physical boundaries of the area should be determined and, preferably, listed by sectional and township codes and mapped. Then, as you work with each source, you can check off each quarter and section as information is transcribed, and avoid duplication of effort.

The fourth step is to decide what time period is going to be covered, down to the decade at least. Most researchers will probably be interested in unravelling the history of the original disposition of the land. In most of southern Manitoba this would mean starting about 1870 or 1880 and carrying through to about 1910 or 1920, or whenever most of the area finally ended up in the hands of settlers. In the north and northwest, the period from about 1890 to 1920 or 1930 would be of particular interest. While the period chosen may be altered somewhat in the course of research, it is important to have "working" dates beforehand; and it is better to overestimate slightly, than the reverse.

Having determined time and area, the next question is how detailed the research will be. To a certain extent the answer to this will depend on the dimensions of the first two factors. Also important are the resources of the researchers. In general, a larger area and a longer time period will reduce the detail that can be handled. Simply finding out the disposition of the lands in nine or ten townships and the names of and dates for the original settlers, for twenty or thirty years, could be a major project. To get complete lists and details — including private sales and transfers — for an area of any size would require considerable time and effort. Given that the information sought is available (somewhere!), the main stumbling block to completion is the amount of time and the number of people available for research.

One of the biggest problems faced in "group" research projects is co-ordination. When several people are working with the same material, it is absolutely essential that the same type of information be regularly transcribed, and that it be done in a common format. There are several ways in which this can be accomplished, but perhaps the simplest is to have a central filing system for all information. One person or a small committee would have charge of a master file consisting of one card or looseleaf sheet for each quarter section (or whatever basic unit is involved). The director(s) would be responsible for reviewing each source beforehand to see what data would be of use, setting up a format of transcription, and later having relevant information transcribed onto the master cards or pages. At the same time the source of each piece of information should be noted, using either a colour or letter code. This will enable dubious data to be checked at a later date, if necessary. It should be pointed out that, rather than copying each source in its entirety on the master card, the collator can save time and energy by using new sources to supplement and correct older ones. That is, you need only put supplemental data on the master cards after the first entry or two, while also taking careful note of the sources which confirm existing information. A colour or letter code is also useful in this. With practice, and by trial and error, a group should soon be able to work out convenient methods, bearing in mind that accuracy should always come before simplicity.

A large number of sources can be of use in land ownership research but certain basic items are readily accessible and unusually valuable.

Dominion Land Records

Until 1930 all Crown lands in Manitoba were the property of the Dominion government. Records pertaining to homesteads, Dominion land sales, School lands, timber and grazing permits, parish lands, military and Metis grants, and sundry lesser grants and permits were kept and held by the federal Department of the Interior. A numbered file was maintained for each piece of land. Into this were put all of the basic legal documents (applications, etc.) and correspondence relating to land. In the case of a normal homestead quarter-section these documents would include an entry application, a form requesting permission to patent (fiat), and the patent application itself. Forms relating to scrip, cancellation, improvements (where a cancelled homestead was being taken up), and payments might also be included, as might correspondence within the department, with the local Dominion lands agency, and with the settler regarding these matters. Relevant files could also include information relating to the reservation of land for particular purposes (Indian reserves, churches, school sites, rights-of-way, etc.).

In 1930 all unsold Dominion land in Manitoba (and Saskatchewan and Alberta) became the property of the province. The Dominion retained jurisdiction over land entered for the homestead or sale, until such time as it was patented or cancelled (in the latter case it went to the province). The Dominion land records remained in Ottawa until the early 1950s, when they were handed over to the three provinces concerned. Those for Manitoba went to the Crown Lands Branch. A complete microfilming project was begun, which to date has produced some 1300 reels of copied material. Several hundred more, mainly parish land files, should be completed shortly. Unfortunately, the originals of much of the material microfilmed in the 1950s — the better part of the ordinary files — were destroyed, and the microfilm copies are of an extremely low quality, some being nearly illegible. A fairly complete set of original fiats, however, is available at the Crown Lands

Branch. These contain much of the information relating to patents. All of these records are arranged solely by land location.

For information, call the Crown Lands Branch, listed in the telephone directory under Government of Manitoba.

These records should be the main source of information for historical land research in Manitoba, and especially for homestead cancellations, which are seldom recorded elsewhere. However, the low quality of the microfilm copies, the lack of originals, and the shortage of microfilm viewing facilities at the Branch office greatly reduce their usefulness. Large-scale searches involving microfilmed materials would be impractical at present, although "spot checks" of samples and searches for specific information on specific pieces of land would be worthwhile. If the searchers have access to another microfilm reader, they might consider purchasing copies of the relevant rolls of records for their area for examination at leisure. The cost is nominal (about $5 per roll) and the purchase can be arranged at the Crown Lands Branch.

Township / Patent Diagrams

Township diagrams are maps of townships drawn from the original surveyor's notes showing local features at the time of survey. (This information may be supplemented by the actual notes, available at PAM or the Surveys Branch.) If the maps contain information concerning Dominion grants and patents, they are known as patent diagrams. For Dominion-controlled unreserved lands, the type of transaction involved in granting a patent is shown (e.g., homestead, pre-sale, sale, military homestead, etc.) with, usually, the name of the person awarded the patent. The same is given for some of the provincial lands. Swamp lands are often identified by the notation "Manitoba Govt. Order-in Council," with the date. School lands are often identified only if sold, with the notation M.S.L. Sale or S.L. Sale, and left blank otherwise. For corporate land grants the name of the company is usually given and, occasionally, in the case of the CPR, the name of a purchase. Note that the numbers given for HBC and CPR lands are those assigned by the Dominion to the transfer of the grant. They are not consecutive contract numbers, unlike those given for Dominion land transfers. Many CPR lands are shown as patented to the CPR in 1901. This means that they were unsold (or that the sale contract had not been completed), when the CPR's twenty-year tax exemption ran out. The information on the patent diagrams is often incomplete, especially in the case of corporate lands. Moreover, where it is given it can be misleading. Note, for instance, that only successful, completed homestead and sale contracts are shown. The patent diagrams do not show previous uncompleted and cancelled contracts (except, indirectly, in the case of 80-acre homesteads). Also, they do not show the dates for contract entry or completion for any of the transfers. In the case of Dominion sales, pre-emptions are not always differentiated from ordinary sales. In short, patent diagrams are generally useful in showing the disposition of lands, but are not too reliable regarding disposals.

For *information*, call the Surveys and Mapping Branch, listed in the telephone directory under Government of Manitoba.

Land Titles Registry

Land titles in Manitoba are filed under two different systems (see Appendix 3 for further detail). The first is the abstract system, in which entries under the Registry Act of 1870 are filed. Summaries of transactions concerning the land are written in "abstract books" by quarter-section. Dates, names and prices are usually given. The original papers are available if necessary. The second system files titles under the Real Property Act of 1885. This system does not use abstract books. In order to research transactions it is necessary to go through the files of Certificates of Title for each lot or quarter-section and extract your own "abstract" list. Note that any piece of land can have been registered under either Act completely, or under both, changing over at some time. The change is usually from the Registry to the Real Property Act where it occurs, and note of it is made in the abstract book.

Like patent diagrams, title registries record only completed transfers, where title to the land changed hands. They do not show when the contract was started or indicate uncompleted contracts. Further, they do not usually show the type of contract involved (i.e., a Dominion land homestead or sale, or a corporate sale), but this can generally be deduced from other entries in the file. When using abstract books and Real Property Act Certificates of Title, references to such items as "liens" and "quit claims" can be ignored for all intents and purposes. Focus on patent and title listings. Note that entries in the abstract books are not always in chronological order, so a quick glance up and down the column of dates, before transcribing anything, is in order.

For *information*, call the Land Titles Office, listed in the telephone directory under Government of Manitoba.

Municipal Records

There are several types of municipal documents which can be of use, particularly assessment and collector's rolls. Assessment rolls give the names of land owners and tenants (if any), the taxable value of the property, and the value of exempted property and buildings. Collector's rolls give the actual place of residence of the owner and the school district in which the land is located. Supplementary information, such as summary lists of untaxable and corporate lands is often included. The earlier assessment rolls were usually amended annually for three to five years before a new one was made, whereas collector's rolls were new every year. Other municipal records of interest are the minutes of the Municipal Council, voters' lists, and population records. These often contain information concerning land tenure and use.

The earlier records of many municipalities have been destroyed, lost, or misplaced. Where available they can be invaluable. A search of the local municipal office, with the assistance of the staff of course, is certainly worth the time and effort. Ask the clerk or secretary-treasurer to explain the original purpose of the document. This will help you to decide how complete and reliable it is, and what use you can make of it. Generally speaking, the information in municipal documents is quite reliable, but it tends to be fragmented or inconsistently recorded. Also, of course, it may be incomplete for the purpose which you have in mind. The assessment and collector's taxation rolls are probably the most useful, in that they give a complete record of land holdings for and over a specific period. Therefore, the more of them available, the better.

For information, call the municipal office. Permission of the local council may be required for use.

Tyman Records

This is the material on which J.L. Tyman's doctoral dissertation and book (*By Section, Township and Range*) were based. It includes complete transcriptions of original records of the disposition and disposal of farm lands in western Manitoba. The bibliography of *By Section, Township and Range* gives a comprehensive list of the original sources. Material is listed by quarter-section (the smallest unit dealt with) and is arranged by type of grant (i.e. Dominion lands, School, provincial, CPR, HBC, etc.), with some special categories, such as squatters lands. For most grants, dates for entries and the start of sales contracts are given as well as dates of patent and title transfer. For the corporate grants, details of some cancelled sales as well as successful ones are provided. Names of buyers for HBC lands, however, are lacking. In several instances sale prices are given and contract notes are appended, as in the case of CPR cultivation rebates.

For the study of land ownership in western Manitoba, the Tyman transcriptions are indispensable. They bring together information from many sources, some of which are not available in Manitoba in a simplified format. This means that special research skills are not required to make use of them. Their main drawbacks are that they cover only the disposition and first disposal of the land (i.e. to a settler), and that they deal exclusively with farm lands and never touch urban townsite land records. Dr. Tyman's *By Section, Township and Range* should be studied carefully before and while making use of the records since direct reference is made to them, and the book as a whole provides a context for their understanding and application.

The Tyman Records are located at the Geography Department of Brandon University. Permission to use the material must be obtained from the Department.

Other Records

It is fair to say that in researching land ownership you never know what can be useful or what will turn up. One source which should be examined is the various lists of lands which were periodically issued by the governments and the companies holding land. The Provincial Library and the Provincial Archives in Winnipeg have a certain number of these on file. J.L. Tyman's bibliography will give some idea of what is available, while a letter to the Public Archives of Canada outlining your subject area might produce unexpected dividends. "Settlement propaganda" of this type often contains useful information about conditions at the time of settlement in a specific area.

Another potential source is a community newspaper, which might contain editorial commentaries on local conditions and lists or advertisements of land sales.

Last, but not least, check your own area for original diaries, letters, or other records kept by the first settlers. These often have comments on the specific problems of procuring and settling land in the area which can be used to fill gaps in, or to supplement information from other sources.

Collection of this broad range of information for each quarter-section, or a sample of quarter-sections, in the district will permit precise analysis of the settlement process. The record of each type of disposition can be examined, for example, to determine the importance and price of HBC, CPR, school, and pre-emption sales in the district as compared to Metis scrip, military grants, and homestead grants. Changes in disposal policies can also be discovered (for example, what are the consequences when a private colonization company decides to sell its holdings?). Thus, a general chronology of the disposition (by grant type) and ultimate disposal of the lands in one district can be constructed. The three factors of price, quality, and site (that is, site as determined by such factors as proximity to services, to neighbours, or to preferred landscape), will be prominent in this analysis. Did settlers prefer low-priced lands, regardless of place or convenience, or did service and convenience factors predominate? Did this pattern change over time?

It is also possible to analyse individual settlers in many districts. Local histories and various church and municipality records will supplement the information in the land records, often giving the settler's country of origin, age, family size and religion, as well as the size of his farm and the settlement strategies (funds invested, whether homestead, purchase or pre-emption) that he pursued.

GLOSSARY OF TERMS USED IN LAND TITLE RESEARCH IN MANITOBA

NOTE: Terms printed in italics are defined in the glossary.

ABANDONED HOMESTEAD: A *homestead* on which *conditions* were not met, deserted by the enterer. Became open for a new homestead entry, an *eighty-acre homestead* entry or for a *Dominion Land sale*. Many were so abandoned after the *boom* of 1881-82.

ABSTRACT BOOK: The means of recording *title* to land under the *Registry Act*. The book contains a chronological record of each title to land, indicating the substance of all facts appearing on public records which affect the title. Abbreviated entries refer to documents on file. Titles registered may not be absolute.

ALIENATION: The transfer of the property and possession of land from one party to another. Usually refers to transfers by the Crown.

ASSESSMENT (ROLL), MUNICIPAL: Most municipal income is derived from a tax on land. Every spring municipalities appoint assessors who evaluate all assessable property (see *exemption*) and make a complete list of land, other property and owners. Taxes are then levied on a percentage basis (rates) determined by the municipal council. Assessment rolls provide a very valuable complete list of land holdings, although assessment figures are not always representative of actual market value. See *collector's roll*.

ASSIGNMENT: The transfer of property or any rights therein to another. In land research, usually refers to the allocation of title to a second party before homestead or sale conditions are actually completed. Title went to the second party on completion. This method was often used by *speculators*.

BELTS, DOMINION LAND: Term referring to the status of a given area of land in reference to its distance from a railway line. The plan of 1879 involved the sale of *Dominion Lands* to support government-built railways, with prices of *sales* and availability of free *homesteads* varying directly with distance from the lines. With the CPR Charter of 1881, Dominion Lands belts were retained, but they affected only the price of *pre-emptions* and ordinary sales. See also *mile belt reserve* and *forty-eight mile belt*.

BLOCK: Legal subdivision comprised of *lots* in villages, towns, and cities.

BLOCK OUTLINE: First stage of sectional survey system surveying, whereby *township* outlines were established. See *subdivision* and *survey*.

BOOM: Period of rapid settlement, railway construction, and speculation. Manitoba had two main booms, in 1881-82 and 1896-1912 (approximately).

BOUNDARY COMMISSION TRAIL: Road laid out in 1872-73 along the 49th Parallel for the use of surveyors marking the boundary. Also used by North-West Mounted Police in 1874, and by many settlers in the south and southwest before the construction of the railway (1884).

CANCELLATION: Termination of land sales contract or homestead entry because of the failure of purchaser or enterer to make payments or fulfil conditions on time. Land was then revested in the owning agency and was usually re-opened for sale or entry.

CARLTON TRAIL: Old cart trail used by HBC and Metis cart brigades, running from Red River, north of the Assiniboine, to Fort Ellice. A southern branch ran south of the Assiniboine towards Wood Mountain, and was paralleled by the CPR line in 1881. Both trails were heavily used by settlers after 1870.

COLLECTOR'S ROLL: Duplications of municipal *assessment rolls* for rate-collection purposes, which also give the actual residence of the property owner, and the *school district* to which land belonged. Lists of untaxable land are often included, as are consolidated lists of corporate holdings (e.g., CPR).

Collector's rolls are usually annual, whereas assessment rolls are often simply corrected for several years at a time. Both are useful for research, if available.

COLONIZATION COMPANIES: Business enterprises bringing in settlers to a specific area in return for a price reduction on *Dominion Lands* for the company (e.g., Shell River Colony).

COLONIZATION RAILWAYS: Private railway companies for which Dominion and provincial government subsidies took the form of an option to buy adjacent lands at the reduced price of $1 per acre.

COLONIZATION SOCIETIES: Organized groups of settlers settling together in a specific area in return for special privileges from the Dominion Government (e.g., Souris Sowden settlement).

CONDITIONS, CULTIVATION, AND RESIDENCE: Requirements imposed for the fulfilment of *sale* or *homestead contract* in lieu of or in addition to money. These varied, but usually a homesteader had to live on or near his land, build a house, and cultivate a specified acreage in order to get his *patent*. On some sales, the CPR offered a *rebate* of half the purchase price for cultivating a certain acreage of the land within a specific time. The purpose of these measures was to give an advantage to actual settlers and discourage *speculators*.

CONTRACT: A legal agreement to fulfil monetary and/or other conditions in return for land (e.g., a homestead or sale). A *patent* or *title* was not awarded until these terms were met.

CONVEYANCE: The deed or instrument other than a will whereby an interest in property is transferred by one person to another (see *alienation, patent, title*).

COUNTY SYSTEM: System of local government attempted in the early 1880s, consisting of several very large administrative units on the Ontario and American models. Impractical at the time due to primitive communication systems, and replaced in 1884 by *rural municipalities*. In many cases, however, the county names remained in use for some time afterwards.

CROWN LAND: All land in a province not otherwise granted or alienated. Administered by the provincial government in all provinces except Manitoba, Saskatchewan, and Alberta, where they belonged to the Dominion. These provinces did not gain possession until 1930 (see *Dominion land*).

DISPOSAL: Sale, giving away, or any other disposition of land. In land research this term is used to refer to the passing of land from the Dominion, or from a corporate body in possession of a Dominion land grant, to an individual or corporation.

DISPOSITION: The parting with or giving up of property. In land research this term refers to the manner in which Dominion lands were apportioned into different categories: i.e. the allocation of *grants* and reserves by the Dominion government (e.g. *homestead* and sale lands, *School land,* HBC and CPR grant lands, etc.).

DOMINION LANDS: Land owned and administered by the federal government. All *Crown land* in Manitoba was Dominion land under the terms of the Manitoba Act of 1870, although the Dominion later gave some land to the province in the form of the *Manitoba university* and *swamp land grants.* The balance of Crown lands remaining undisposed was transferred to the province in 1930.

DOMINION LANDS BRANCH: Office of the federal Department of the Interior responsible for the administration of agricultural *Dominion lands,* and thus in charge of *homesteads* and *sales.* Other branches were responsible for timber and grazing lands, surveys, etc. The internal organization of the department changed several times.

"DOMINION LANDS" POLICY: A blanket term covering federal policies governing the *disposition* and *disposal* of *Dominion Lands* in the West. This had two main purposes: the promotion of rapid and effective settlement and the construction of railways.

EIGHTY-ACRE HOMESTEADS: A form of *homestead* entry on cancelled 160-acre homesteads in the period 1883-86. Half was taken as a homestead, half as a *pre-emption* sale. All *improvements* previously made on the land were given to the new enterer for an extra $5 fee. These are very useful as indicators of previous homestead cancellations which might not otherwise be recorded.

ENTRY: On taking up a *homestead* an applicant had to make an entry for it, stating that he or she had not previously filed for one (exception: see *second entry*). This entry bound him or her to the homestead *conditions* required at the time, and gave the right to *patent* the land once they were fulfilled. *Pre-emption* entries were also made at this time.

EXEMPTIONS (TAXATION): Buildings on improved land, farm machinery and stock, and personal effects and household goods are all exempt from municipal taxation (see *assessment* and *collector's rolls*).

FIAT: The application form filled out by a homesteader as the first step in applying for *patent*. In essence, an application for an inspection of the land to confirm that homestead *improvements* had been made and other *conditions* met, (see *homestead inspector*).

FORTY-EIGHT MILE BELT: The area for 24 miles (three townships) on each side of the CPR main line, reserved in 1881, in which the company was supposed to select its grant lands from the odd-numbered sections. In the event the area was not large enough to provide the 25 million acres, especially since the land chosen had to be "fairly fit for settlement," and the company had to go further afield to find enough. The price of land was affected by its position in the belt relative to the rail line. See also *mile belt reserve* and *belts, dominion land*.

GRANT: A certain area and/or quantity of land allocated and reserved by the Dominion for a specific purpose. (e.g., CPR grant, *School Land, Swamp Land Grant*, etc.). The process of subdividing Dominion Lands in this fashion is referred to as *disposition*.

GRAZING LEASE: *Dominion lands* rented from the government for grazing purposes. Terms and rates varied over time.

GROUP SETTLEMENTS: Ethnic groups settling in large numbers in a specific area. Such settlements were often sponsored by charitable organizations, railway or land companies, and given special rates or conditions on corporate or Dominion lands. The term is usually used to refer to non-Anglophone minority groups (see, for example, *reserves*).

HOMESTEAD: About half of the *Dominion Lands* in Manitoba were reserved for 160-acre "free" homesteads and associated *pre-emptions* and *sales*. A settler would select a vacant quarter, file an *entry* for it at the nearest Dominion Lands Office, and pay a $10 registration fee. If *improvements* had previously been made on the land it might be necessary to pay extra, subject to a decision by the Lands Branch in Ottawa. Until 1889 the settler could also file for a *pre-emption* on an adjacent quarter-section. In order to gain final possession of the land, a settler had to fulfil certain residence and cultivation *conditions*, theoretically within three years. After this had been done, a *fiat* was filed and the work was checked by a local *homestead inspector*. If all was in order the settler then received the *patent* (*title*) to the land from the Dominion, and might then officially begin the process of acquiring the pre-emption, if any. The homestead and pre-emption regulations were changed several times, but generally stayed within this framework.

HOMESTEAD INSPECTOR: An official of the *Dominion Lands Branch* responsible for investigating settlers' applications for patents for their *homesteads* and *pre-emptions*. When they thought that all *conditions* had been met, settlers filed a *fiat* stating so with the local Dominion Lands Office, and the inspector then checked to see that the necessary residence, cultivation and construction conditions had been complied with.

IMPROVEMENTS: Work done adding value to land, such as buildings, cultivation, etc. Persons entering for *homesteads* with previous improvements usually had to pay extra, as was also the case for most sales. Both the Dominion, for homesteads, and the CPR, in return for *rebates* on some sales, demanded that the settler make improvements as part of the contract.

INCORPORATION: *Municipalities* (rural, village, town or city) are "corporate" entities. This means that they have a Charter from the Crown giving them a legal existence and rights, such as levying certain taxes within their jurisdiction to make improvements and maintain community property (such as roads). A village, town or city can become a municipality in its own right, or can advance up the "scale" of municipal levels, if it has the requisite population and assessable property. Municipal organization, rights, and duties are regulated by provincial legislation.

LAND COMPANIES: Private corporations investing in and dealing in land, a block of which was often purchased from the Dominion or from a railway company. For example, the Canada North-West Land Company purchased a large portion of the CPR main line grant in the early 1880s.

LAND TITLE OFFICE: Provincial office maintaining land ownership records and issuing titles. All land in the province is covered, with one office in each Land Titles District (e.g. Winnipeg, Brandon, Dauphin). Records under both the *Registry Act* and the *Real Property Act* are kept.

LIEN (CHARGING LIEN): There are many different kinds of liens. The most common one dealing with land is the charging lien. This involves the right to charge property in another's possession with the payment of a debt. It constitutes a form of encumbrance under the *Real Property Act*.

LOT: A 40-acre unit of the sectional survey system. The sixteen lots in a section are independently numbered. The term may also be used to refer to rectangular *timber lots,* townsite lots, and *river lots.*

MANITOBA UNIVERSITY GRANT: A land grant of 150,000 acres set aside in 1885 by the Dominion to support the University of Manitoba.Most of the land was selected in 1890 but, because of administrative and political problems, was not handed over to the university until 1898. Sales were administered by the Provincial Lands Department and the University Board, with proceeds going towards university capital expenditures and operating costs. About 70 percent of the land was located in western Manitoba.

METIS SCRIP: The Manitoba Act of 1870 reserved 1,400,000 acres of *Dominion Lands* in Manitoba for the Red River Metis. *Scrip* for 1,448,160 acres was eventually issued, but much ended up in the hands of *speculators* since the scrip was negotiable as cash.

MILE BELT RESERVE: *Dominion lands* sections adjacent to the CPR main line were withdrawn from *homestead* entry in 1882 until CPR station locations were decided upon. The purpose of this was to forestall *speculators*. The belt was opened to homesteading in 1884, but the size of individual acquisitions was restricted.

MILITARY HOMESTEAD: Several different allotments of *Dominion lands* were made to ex-military personnel. Soldiers in the Wolseley Expedition of 1870, and those serving in the Winnipeg garrison between 1871 and 1877, were entitled to a 160-acre *homestead* without *conditions*. Government veterans of the 1885 Rebellion were given a choice between a warrant for $80 or scrip exchangeable for 320 acres of land. Those taking the scrip (which could also be sold or transferred) received a free 320-acre homestead, subject to the usual residence and cultivation conditions for a 160-acre one. Some scrip was also issued to Canadian volunteers returning from the Boer War (1899-1902). North-West Mounted Policemen who joined before 1879 were also entitled to a free 160-acre homestead after three years of service. See also *Soldier Settlement Board*.

MINUTES: Records of meetings of school boards, municipal councils, etc. Municipal minutes often contain copies of annual budget estimates and minutes of courts of revision for the *assessment rolls* (municipal councils also act as Courts of Revision to hear appeals against assessments.) *Tax Sales* and other municipal business related to lands may also be included.

MORTGAGE: A charge on land as security for payment of a loan or debt. Under the *Registry Act* the creditor has possession of the *title* to the land, subject to repayment. Under the *Real Property Act* the owner retains the title unless he or she fails to fulfil the contract. The mortgage constitutes a charge on the title in this situation.

MUNICIPALITY: A municipality is a specific area with its own separate government. Included are *rural municipalities*, villages, towns (with populations over 500), and cities (with populations over 10,000), Most municipal officers are elected and appointed on the basis of *ward* representation. See also *incorporation*.

NOTIFICATION: The Hudson's Bay Company received its land grant lands automatically on "notification" from the *Dominion Lands Branch* that the land had been *subdivided* (sections 8 and all or part of 26 in every township). The company did not have the option of rejecting unsuitable land, although some of the worst was later surrendered to the Dominion.

PATENT (LAND): First title to land issued by the government for some portion of the public domain (*Crown lands*).

PATENT DIAGRAM: See *Township Diagram.*

PRE-EMPTION (SALE): Sometimes referred to as a "presale" in documents. This was an interim entry for a *quarter-section adjacent to a homesteaded quarter, separately filed for at the time of the homestead entry.* If the homestead *conditions* were completed, the settler was allowed to buy the pre-emption. The price was artificially low (usually $1 per acre) and time-payment was allowed. The right of pre-emption was discontinued at the end of 1889 (this did not affect settlers with uncompleted entries).

PROVINCIAL LANDS (MANITOBA): Under the Manitoba Act of 1870 all *Crown lands* in Manitoba were the property of the Dominion, leaving the province without any lands to sell for revenue. To partially correct this, the *Swamp Land Grant* and the *Manitoba University Grant* were given to the province by the Dominion in 1885. Unsold swamp lands were taken back by the Dominion in

1911, when an arrangement to give Manitoba a cash subsidy was reached. Manitoba finally gained control of what was left of the Crown lands in 1930.

PUBLIC SHOOTING GRANT: Lands, usually marsh or swamp, open to the public for hunting.

QUARTER-SECTION: A 160-acre unit of the sectional survey (1/4 mile square). This was the basic unit of the land disposal system, most homesteads and sales being of this size.

QUIT CLAIM: A legal agreement in which an individual or corporation gives up all claims to a particular piece of land; used to transfer titles under the *Registry Act*.

REAL PROPERTY ACT: New Act passed in 1885 for registration of land *titles* in Manitoba, supplementing the *Registry Act* of 1870. Under the new system, which was based on that introduced in Australia by Sir Robert Torrens, a Certificate of Title is provided for each piece of land registered under the act. Titles are completely investigated by the *Land Titles Office* before a certificate is issued, and this usually constitutes final and absolute evidence of ownership. Registration under the act is optional, but most urban and about 90 per cent of surveyed rural land in the province now comes under it. A single-title file record system is used.

REBATES: The CPR, by previous arrangement on some sales, made rebates of up to one-half of the purchase price of the land in return for the fulfilment of certain cultivation conditions. Sales without these conditions were usually higher priced.

REGISTRY ACT: An act passed in 1870 for the registration of Manitoba land titles, based on English property law. There is no obligation to register relevant documents at a *Land Title Office*, and those registered only constitute evidence of title. A complete investigation is required to gain a clear title to a piece of land, involving the clearance of all "clouds" on it. An "abstract" system of file records is used. About 10 per cent of the surveyed rural land in the province is still registered under this act, the balance being under the *Real Property Act*.

RESERVATIONS, INDIAN: Lands set aside by treaty (or, in the case of the Manitoba Sioux, by a negotiated agreement) for native tribes, and held in trust in perpetuity by the Dominion government. The last treaty for Manitoba was signed in 1875. Most reservations were assigned and occupied before the arrival of white settlers, and were automatically set aside on being surveyed.

RESERVES, EAST AND WEST: Dominion lands set aside for Russian Mennonite *group settlements*. The East Reserve, north and east of the Rat River, was assigned in 1874; the West Reserve, west of the Red along the US border, in 1876. These are notable for the European village patterns which were imposed on the sectional *survey* system.

RIVER LOT: A form of Manitoba land survey and tenure used along the lower Red and Assiniboine rivers, similar to that of Quebec. The lots usually consisted of a ten-chain (660 foot) river frontage and a strip reaching two miles back. The owner could also acquire a further two miles of "hay privilege." An attempt to replace this system with the sectional survey in 1869 was a partial cause of the Insurrection. In the end it was retained, with the new system starting where the river lots ended; although the lot numbering system used before 1870 was changed.

ROAD ALLOWANCE: Strips left between *sections* in *townships* for the construction of roads. The First System of *survey*, used in most of southern Manitoba, had a complete grid of 99-foot wide allowances. The Third System, used mainly in the northwest of the province, had allowances on every second east-west line and all of the north-south ones. These were 66 feet wide. Road allowances are municipal property.

RURAL MUNICIPALITY: A *municipal* government area comprised of one or more *townships*. Each RM has its own elected reeve, a councillor from each *ward*, and an appointed secretary-treasurer. RM's replaced the *county system* in 1884.

SALE, DOMINION LAND: *Dominion Land* sales were unconditional cash or term sales, similar to private sales. Some restrictions on the amount which could be purchased by any individual were imposed. Prices were generally low, varying with the distance from a railway. These sales were not particularly important in Manitoba until 1890, when *pre-emptions* were cut off. One feature of Dominion land sales was that some purchasers were allowed to convert their sales contract into a homestead entry, and vice versa.

SCHOOL LAND GRANT: Two sections per township (11 and 29) were set aside by the Dominion in 1872 "as an endowment for the purposes of education." They were under the control of the Dominion, but sales revenue went to the province, in trust. The land was held off the market until a high price could be gotten for it, public auctions being the usual method of disposal. The unsold balance of the grant came under provincial control in 1930.

SCHOOL DIVISION: Areas within *municipalities* supporting schools. These are financed by school taxes,and special school levies on ratepayers. The rates are established and the taxes collected by the municipality; expenditures and policy are directed by a school board of ratepayers for each district, subject to the approval of the council. Most small rural districts have been replaced by centralized consolidated school divisions. Manitoba school districts are numbered in the chronological order of their appearance. Note that there is no direct connection between the *School Land Grant* and local schools.

SCRIP: A means of granting land without specifying the actual place of settlement. Scrip was a warrant for *Dominion Land*, and could usually be sold or exchanged freely. Land scrip was issued to Selkirk settler families in 1876, to the Metis (see *Metis scrip*), and veterans (see *military homestead*).

SECOND HOMESTEAD ENTRY: Between 1882 and 1889, settlers were permitted to enter for a second *homestead*. Theoretically this was to allow a settler a second try if the first was a failure, but the right was often abused.

SECTION: A 640-acre unit of the sectional *survey*, one mile square. Thirty-six numbered sections make up a *township*.

SOLDIER GRANT: See *Soldier Settlement Board.*

SOLDIER SETTLEMENT BOARD: An agency set up to administer the allotment of Dominion land "Soldier Grants" to veterans of World War One. Some of these were free homesteads with supplementary loans, while some consisted of loans to purchase improved farms. The settlers were closely supervised by the board. Since little good quality land remained available in Manitoba at this time, a high rate of failure resulted. Most Soldier Grants in this province were located in the northwest.

SPECULATOR: A person or organization buying or entering for land with no intention of actually settling on or cultivating it. The land was held until the value rose. The Dominion and the CPR, among others, attempted to discourage speculators by attaching *conditions* to *homestead* and *sale* contracts. The term is often applied loosely.

SQUATTER: A person settling on land before the *survey*. Most squatters later received normal homestead rights to their land (adjusted as a quarter-section) even when it conflicted with other grants (e.g., CPR, School lands).

SUBDIVISION: The second stage of the *survey*, in which *block outlines* of *townships* were divided into *sections, quarter-sections, lots,* etc. This was a necessary prelude to settlement since the legal definition of land units was required for the allocation of *grants*.

SURVEY (SECTIONAL SURVEY SYSTEM): The process of dividing land into standard-sized units. In Manitoba this was based on six-mile-square *townships* made up of 36 one-mile-square *sections*. Two different systems of survey were used. The First System of 1871 was used in most of southern Manitoba. It provided a complete grid of 99-foot wide *road allowances* in each township. Accuracy was often sacrificed for speed, with errors being allowed to accumulate in the westernmost sections of the townships. These, typically, are somewhat smaller than the rest. The Third System of 1881 was used north of Duck Mountain in the northwest, and provided a partial grid of 66-foot wide road allowances in each township. As a result, these were slightly smaller than those in the First System, but errors were spread evenly through all 36 sections. The Second System was not used in Manitoba. Fractional Townships were used to fill the gaps where the First and Third System townships met and did not coincide. Most of these are found north of the Township 26 line. Other partial townships are found bordering the old *river lots* along the lower Red and Assiniboine rivers. Note that all Manitoba townships are numbered by their position west or east of the Principal Meridian (W1 or E1), a north-south baseline running between Winnipeg and Portage la Prairie.

SURVEYOR'S NOTES: Narrative notes kept by *Dominion lands* surveyors. These often provide detailed information on *squatters*, topography, soils, vegetation, trails, and other matters of contemporary interest. The descriptions are often the earliest detailed account of a specific area, and can be used to clarify and expand upon the information given on *township diagrams*.

SWAMP LAND GRANT: In 1885 the Dominion government granted Manitoba all swamp and marsh *Dominion lands* in the province. These were to be sold for revenue. About two million acres of land were handed over, most being selected under a Manitoba Order-in-Council issued in 1891. The unsold balance of the swamp lands reverted to the Dominion in 1911, and some was later opened for homesteading. All Dominion lands in Manitoba reverted to the province in 1930. Note that, due to a loose definition of "swamp" in the 1885 agreement, some of the land involved turned out to be fairly good. See also *Manitoba University Grant.*

TAX SALE: The sale of lands by a *municipality* to recover unpaid taxes. The total taxes owing constituted a reserve price, and if this was not offered, the municipality itself became the owner.

TITLE: Under the *Real Property Act* ownership is guaranteed; under the *Registry Act* it is conditional. A thorough title search must be made before an absolute title can be claimed.

TOWNSHIP: A unit of the sectional *survey* system: 36 square miles (23,040 acres). Manitoba townships are numbered by their position in horizontal rows of townships running north from the 49th parallel (those along the boundary are all numbered "1"), and by their position in vertical columns of townships ("ranges") running east or west away from the Principal Meridian (those along the meridian are numbered "1"). See also *block outline, subdivision.*

TOWNSHIP DIAGRAM: Official maps of each township issued by the *Dominion Lands Branch.* The diagrams are based on *surveyor's notes,* and show *subdivision,* true acreage and some terrain features. "Patent diagrams" are those on which Dominion grants and patents have been transcribed. They are not always accurate or complete.

TRANSFER: An act by which the *title* to property is conveyed from one person to another. Note that, when the Dominion transferred its lands to the company grants (e.g., CPR, HBC), it did not usually give them a *patent* for the lands. Rather, the first title was issued to the first buyer of the land by the Dominion. In theory, the company grant lands were *Dominion lands* assigned to the company for *disposal.* In practice, statute law gave the companies the equivalent of a title to the lands.

WARDS: Administrative subdivisions of *municipalities.* Most rural *municipalities* have between four and six. Each ward elects one or more councillors (based on population) to a two-year term on the council. They direct municipal affairs, and are responsible for expenditures within their own ward. Assessment rates can vary from ward to ward, depending on the specific requirements and resources of each.

WOOD LOTS: Forested lands set aside during the survey to provide wood for settlers. *Quarter-sections* were divided into *lots* of twenty acres (330 feet by 1/4 mile). Between 1872 and 1874 these were given free on a "first come, first served" basis. After 1874 the price was raised to $1 per acre, and in 1879 to $2.50. In 1881 the price was set at $5 per acre. These wood supplies were necessary for settlers because timber could not be cut on a *homestead* or *pre-emption* (or on most *sale* lands) until the patent was issued.

PRINCIPAL SOURCES

Black, H.C. *Black's Law Dictionary* (St. Paul, Minn.: West Publishing Co., Rev. 4th ed., 1968)

Burke, John *Osborn's Concise Law Dictionary* (London: Sweet & Maxwell, 6th ed., 1976)

Martin, Chester *"Dominion Lands" Policy* L.H. Thomas, ed. (Toronto: McClelland and Stewart, Carleton Library ed., 1973)

Morton, W.L. *Manitoba: A History* (Toronto: University of Toronto Press, 2nd ed., 1967)

Pridham, E.A. "The Title to Land in Manitoba." *Papers Read Before the Historical and Scientific Society of Manitoba* III: 15 (1958), pp. 7-26

Tyman, John L. *By Section, Township and Range: Studies in Prairie Settlement* (Brandon, Man.: Assiniboine Historical Society, 1972)

Agricultural Capability Ratings

D.M. LOVERIDGE

The preceding appendix on land and settlement records is intended to show the ways and means of doing interpretive research using these sources of information. Most land title research done by local historians tends to appear in print as a simple list or map of homesteaders. While such material is certainly of interest, by itself it adds little to the final history and so hardly repays the effort involved. Assuming that a local historian intends to correct this situation by following some of the suggestions made above, it is probable that he or she will soon come up against a further problem, one arising from the simple fact that land records tell far more about the land disposal system than they do about the specific nature of the land itself. Yet the nature of the land was, obviously, an important factor in the process of land disposal.

A settler entering for a homestead or purchasing other land did so, in the majority of cases, for the purpose of establishing him or herself as a farmer. The type and quality of the land chosen was usually more important than its quantity, and certainly more so than the method of acquisition involved. The latter was a means to an end, not an end in itself. When studying the settlement of a small area it is therefore necessary to include the type and quality of the land in the analysis. Doing so, however, can be very difficult. One must consider climate, drainage, topography, soils and vegetation, among other things. Moreover, the settler may have been restricted in the type of farming which the economic situation or other factors allowed him to pursue, and those open to him may not have permitted the optimum type of land use for the area in question. The task of assigning "quality" is obviously a complex one, and most students will quite rightly approach it with caution. For this type of research, however, some form of a simplified scale of land quality, which conforms with other research materials being employed, is necessary.

Fortunately, the means of preparing such a tool are at hand, and in a form which does not necessarily require the specialized knowledge noted above.

The Canada Land Inventory (hereafter cli) is an ongoing project of the Lands Directorate of the Canada Department of Environment. Its purpose is to analyse the capabilities of lands in southern Canada to support various economic activities and renewable resources, including agriculture, forestry, recreation, and wildlife (ungulates and waterfowl). Based on the limitations or assets affecting each activity, a common scale of possible use has been drawn up, and is applied uniformly to the whole of the country. That is, the soil capability for agriculture of lands in New Brunswick, for example, is assessed on the same scale as those in Manitoba. Colour-coded maps are issued in 1:250,000 and 1:1,000,000 scales. In the first, about sixteen map areas, with five topical mapsheets for each area, are relevant to Manitoba, while the second covers the whole of the province with one mapsheet for each topic.

The item of particular interest here is the "Soil Capability for Agriculture" map series in 1:250,000 scale. Each mapsheet covers a rectangular area of about 70 by 90 miles (12 x 15 townships). The detailed base map shows townships and sections, physical features (rivers, lakes, etc.), cities, towns and villages, and roads and rail lines. Superimposed on this is the easily read soil capability assessment. This is made up of eight basic classes, each distinguished by a different colour. The class definitions are based on the intensity of limitations for agriculture, not on the kind of soil alone. Many types of soil could therefore be found in the same class, the assignment depending on their specific capability to support use, rather than on that of the type as a whole. The classes range from class 1, "no significant limitations for use for crops," to class 7, "no capability for arable culture or permanent pasture", with each class in between representing a gradient on the scale. Class 4, for example, denotes "severe limitations that restrict the range of crops (etc.)." In addition to these seven, class 0 covers unclassifiable, non-arable areas such as lakes and bedrock exposures.

Internal variations within these seven main classes are illustrated using nine subclasses, which include adverse climate (c), erosion (e), inundation (i), stoniness (p), shallowness (r), adverse topography (t), excess water (w), other soil limitation (s), and combinations of two or more of these factors which taken together make up a significant restriction (X). These subclasses are used to explain and modify the class ratings. For example, an area designated "3p" would be one with moderately severe limitations to use due to stony soil. Compounds are also possible. An area designated as "6t/e," for example, would be one suitable only for perennial forage crops due to relatively steep hills and erosion. Where classification is more complex, a simple numerical ratio of classes and subclasses present in the area is given. For example, a "3 8/s 5 2/w" rating would mean a mixed area of moderately severe and very severe restrictions due to soil restrictions and excess water, in a proportion of 80 per cent "3s" to 20 per cent "5w". The general rating system, and each of the classes and subclasses, are carefully explained on a "Descriptive Legend" given on each mapsheet. Concise summaries of climate and soils and a short history of agriculture in the area are also provided on each sheet. With these aids, the information presented is readily understandable. In fact, the situation is less complex than it sounds, since most areas contain representatives of only some of the classes and subclasses included in the general scale.

This agricultural capability rating system can become an excellent tool for historical research, with a few simple modifications. It shows both the absolute value of a given piece of farm land, and its value in relation to that around it. By using it in conjunction with settlement and land records, a great deal of information can be had. An analysis might show, for example, that the majority of early settlers took up a specific type of land, regardless of whether it was available as a homestead or for sale, and regardless of price, in the latter case. Or it may show that they took up any type of land in order to be near a town or railway or their family, even though better quality lands were available farther away. On the other hand, it might reveal that the first pioneers took only free homesteads, regardless of quality or location. Any one of these results could have had major repercussions in the future development of the community. At the least, the information will provide a solid basis for your study of agricultural development.

The first step in turning the CLI material into a research tool is to tailor the rating scale to suit your own area and needs. Not all of the classes and subclasses given in the legend may be present on your mapsheet or in your research area. Nor may each class-subclass gradient be relevant by itself. In the R.M. of Sifton, for example, (twps. 7-9, rges. 23-25 W1 inc.; on CLI 62F) only seven classes (2-6 and 0) and three subclasses (i, w, s) are present. Since the main restriction to agriculture in this area was excess water due to poor drainage, it was possible to develop a ten-point scale, as shown in Table I. As can be seen, the general order of CLI classes is maintained, but the severity of water-related problems is used to subdivide them. The new scale is as accurate as the original, but shows the local situation more clearly and is easier to deal with since superfluous data have been removed or subordinated. This approach should be especially useful in areas with compound or ratio classifications or unusual local gradients. The size of your new scale, be it three or fifteen classes, is not important as long as it shows the relevant information for your area and project.

Table 1

Agricultural Capability Rating for Sifton, Manitoba

CLI	Sifton	Description
2i	1	well-drained loam
2w	2	poorly drained loam
3s	3	well-drained sandy loam
4s	4	well-drained sand, level
4w/ws	5	poorly drained sand, seasonal flooding
5s	6	well-drained sand, rolling
5w/ws	7	poorly drained sand, fluctuating marsh
6s	8	sandhills
6w/ws	9	semipermanent marsh
0	10	open water

The second step is to make sure that the CLI map applies to the historical period you are working with. The CLI results are based on modern data, and some changes may have occurred in your area. The basic soil situation will normally be the same, but water levels may have changed, forest cover have been removed, or severe soil drifting and erosion have taken place. These must be accounted for. The best way to do this is to consult the original surveyors' notes and township diagrams (see below), which describe the area as it was before settlement. Compare these with modern topographic maps (1:50,000 scale are best) and air photos (see below). Any changes affecting soil capability should be noted on the CLI map and the area reclassified accordingly. This can be done fairly easily by finding an area on the modern CLI map which corresponds with the altered area as it was in the late 1870s or 1880s, and using that classification for the alteration. An area which is presently dry farm land, for example, may once have been marsh, and therefore the classification given to a similar modern marshy area would be used for it. In most instances, some equivalent area such as this will be found on the modern map. If not, a new rating can easily be drawn up from the data given in the legend. In such a case, the modern class rating for the land would usually remain the same, with the change taking place in the subclass modifier. As long as you are consistent in your reclassification, problems should not arise. In any case, provide a short description of the changes made and your rationale for them.

Once a local scale and an historically accurate map have been prepared, the final step is to mark off your revised 1:250,000 cᴌɪ map (which shows sections as the smallest unit) into quarter-sections. This is necessary because the quarter-section was the basic unit of disposition and disposal, and will therefore be the basic unit in your study. Having done this (pencilled lines are satisfactory, and correctable), a *single* rating from your new scale should be assigned to each quarter-section. This is best done on a larger township map (blank township diagrams on 8-1/2 x 11 sheets are convenient and easy to make). Copy the class boundaries for each township onto this larger map, and write the assigned quarter section values thereon. This gives you a permanent and easily read reference.

While necessary to organize the data, this step can raise problems, nature having no respect for artificial survey systems. It is certain that you will find that some of your quarters will contain elements of two or more classifications. In such cases you have three alternatives:

(1)   make a rule-of-thumb judgment and assign one or the other value;
(2)   assign the values proportionately on a sectional basis;
(3)   Consistently assign the highest (or lowest) value present in the mixture in a substantial quantity.

Option 2 is recommended when working with a large area, since the "averaging" will tend to balance out overall. However, as long as you are consistent, and state the method used, they are equally satisfactory. Once the assignment of values is completed, that for each quarter-section should be noted on the appropriate card or page of your master file of land title data (see appendix 1). From there it can easily be transcribed onto your work sheets, and included in the analysis of chronological or grant disposals.

As is often the case in historical land research, these procedures sound more complex than they actually are. Their use mainly requires careful preparation and common sense in application. The end result, however, can amply repay the modest time required to follow them through. Agricultural capability ratings provide solid and reliable data in an area where generalization and simple guesswork normally reigns.

SOURCES

cᴌɪ maps are available at a nominal price from Canada Map Office, Surveys and Mapping Branch, Energy, Mines and Resources, Ottawa, K1A 0E9. A free index showing the areas covered and the topics covered for each area is available from the same source. Note that the base maps used for the 1:250,000 CLI maps are the National Topographic System maps in the same scale. Therefore if you know the code reference for the latter (e.g. 62F Virden) you know the CLI code and can ask for the CLI map covering that area. Two catalogues of Manitoba maps and air photos are available free from the Surveys Branch office (address above). The office can supply all of the materials listed in them.

For township diagrams and surveyors' notes, see appendix 1, Township/Patent Diagrams.

Photocopies of all air photographs of townships are available for a modest fee from the Surveys and Mapping Branch (see listing under Government of Manitoba in the telephone directory).

Land Records as a Source of Historical Information

ROBERT A. DOYLE

Land records can be of great assistance in historical research. If you are studying a building and want to know who has owned it over the years, land records are an ideal source of information. Similarly, if you are studying the life of one individual and want to know whether he or she owned certain buildings or land, land records may provide the answer.

In Manitoba there are two systems of land registration — the Torrens System under the Real Property Act and the "Old System" under the Registry Act. Since the Real Property Act was passed in 1885, approximately 90 per cent of the settled land in the province has been brought under the operation of this act and the Torrens System of land registration. Thus most research can be conducted by using land titles, the key documents in the Torrens System of land registration.

The Torrens System was not, however, the first system of land registration to be introduced. After Manitoba became a province in 1870, one of the first statutes passed was the Registry Act (R.S.M. 1870, ch R 50). This act introduced what is now referred to as the "Old System" of land registration. Approximately 10 per cent of the settled land in Manitoba is presently registered under this system.

Legal surveys and original township diagrams are other land records which may be of assistance in historical research. They will not help you to discover the ownership of land or buildings; however, they do accurately present the physical features of land at the time it was first surveyed.

---

* I am indebted to Mr. C.A. Evans, District Registrar, Winnipeg Land Titles Office, Winnipeg, Manitoba, for his assistance in the preparation of this appendix.

The central document in the Torrens System of land registration is the land title.

The Face of a Title

There are at least four elements of valuable information on the face of each land title.

1/ Certificate of Title Number. Each certificate of title has a certificate number located on the face of the title in the upper right-hand corner. Under the Torrens System, the history of land cannot be traced without its current certificate of title number(s).

2/ Name(s) of the Owner(s). The name(s) of the owner(s) of a title to land is indicated at the top of the face of the title. Individuals, holding companies, associations or corporations may hold a title to land. When the title is held by individuals, their names, occupations and the village, town, or city in which they reside is indicated. This information is most useful for identifying the owners of a title.

3/ Legal Description of the Land in Full. The legal description is located near the centre of the face of a title. By referring to the legal description of the land, you can be sure that you are tracing the land you intend to trace.

4/ Date of Title. The date on which a title is registered is indicated at the bottom of the face of a title. This is the date an individual, association, or company assumed the ownership of a title to land.

The Back of a Title

There are at least three elements of useful information on the back of each land title.

1/ Previous Certificate of Title Number. The most valuable piece of information for tracing the history of land is located in the upper left-hand corner on the back of a title. It is the previous certificate of title number of the land a researcher is studying.

2/ Transfer of Title Number. Each time a title to land is transferred from one party to another, the transaction is given a transfer number. This number can be helpful in tracing the title to land in cases where the previous certificate of title number on an older title is illegible. However, the previous certificate of title number is usually adequate for finding an earlier title.

3/ Encumbrances. All encumbrances, that is all charges or liabilities relating to land, are listed on the back of a title. Mortgages, caveats, and easements are the most frequently encountered encumbrances. A land title always indicates the type of encumbrance(s), the date it was incurred, and whether or not it has been discharged. If an encumbrance has been discharged, the date of discharge will be indicated.

LAND REGISTRATION UNDER THE REGISTRY ACT

The "Old System" of land registration created by the Registry Act (R.S.M. 1870, ch. R 50), is based on the registration of assurances of title. The accepted conveyance is the Deed of Grant, commonly referred to as a deed. The most useful source of historical information in this system of land registration is the abstract book. These books contain abstracts or short summaries of all transactions that relate to land registered under the Registry Act. Each abstract contains a brief description of the type of transaction, the date it occurred, the names of the parties, and the amount of money involved.

All abstracts of title are indexed according to legal description. If you are studying a building, and have only the address, you can easily obtain the legal description of the land on which the building stands. In a large city, such as Winnipeg or Brandon, the necessary legal description can be obtained by contacting the City's Tax Assessment Department. In a smaller town or village the legal description of the land can be obtained at the local municipal office. Moreover a land title office will often have the necessary material for obtaining the legal description of land. For example in Winnipeg, the Land Titles Office has copies of current tax assessment notices which bear the legal descriptions of the assessable property in that city. (These sources of information may also be used to obtain the legal description and current certificate of title numbers for land registered under the Torrens System.)

With the current legal description, you can turn to the abstract book and find a record of all the legal transactions, that relate to the land in which you are interested. The transactions are entered in the abstract according to the time of registration at the Land Titles Office. They are not necessarily listed in the order in which they occurred, and you may have to rearrange the transactions to follow them in chronological order. If it is necessary, you can obtain a certified copy of all the entries which appear in the abstract.

In most instances, all the information that is required can be obtained by studying the abstract. However you may examine the original deeds described in the abstract simply by taking note of their registration numbers. Each deed is numbered and is filed according to that number and can be located without difficulty.

USING LAND RECORDS TO OBTAIN HISTORICAL INFORMATION

The information available from land records can solve a number of possible problems.

Problem I: You are making a historical study of a building and want to know what individual(s) or organization(s) owned it from the date of its erection. To solve the problem, examine the land records for the land on which the building was standing. If the building had always stood at one location, tracing the ownership of the building would be a simple task. You would need to have only two pieces of information before beginning the tracing process: the present address of the building; and the date it was constructed. The current address would be required in order to obtain the legal description of the land. Land registration under both the Torrens System and the "Old System" is based upon detailed legal descriptions of land.

The date of a building's construction is also necessary as both systems of land records indicate the ownership of land, not the ownership of buildings. Buildings are incidental to the land on which they stand. Thus if it is known that a building was constructed in 1910, it would only be necessary to study the ownership of the land on which the building stands back to 1910 — not to the time of the issuance of a patent (which could possibly be in the late nineteenth century).

If the land was registered under the Torrens System, you would use land titles to trace ownership of the land. If it was registered under the "Old System" you would obtain an abstract of title for the land on which the building stood.

If the building had *not* always stood at one location, the process of tracing the ownership of a building would be far more complicated. In addition to the building's present address and the date of its construction, two more pieces of information would be needed: the previous location(s) of the building; and the date(s) of relocation. As an example, assume a building under study was originally constructed in 1910 at 365 Davidson Street,

Winnipeg. In 1930 it was moved from that location to its present location at 110 Westminster Avenue, Winnipeg.

If the land was registered under the Torrens System, you would: (1) find the legal description and the current certificate of title number for the land at 110 Westminster Avenue; (2) using the previous certificate of title numbers, trace the ownership of land at 110 Westminster Avenue back to 1930; (3) find the legal description and the current certificate of title number for the land at 365 Davidson Street; (4) follow the title of the land at 365 Davidson Street back to 1930, and then trace the ownership of this land from 1930 back to 1910.

If the land was registered under the "Old System" the research would be far less time-consuming. You would: (1) obtain the legal description and then the abstract of title for the land at 110 Westminster Avenue; (2) obtain the legal description and then the abstract of title for the land at 365 Davidson Street; (3) examine the abstract for the land at 110 Westminster Avenue for the period from 1930 to the present day; (4) examine the abstract for the land at 365 Davidson Street for the period from 1910 to 1930.

It is possible that you may not be working solely with Land Titles under the Torrens System or an abstract of titles under the "Old System." The land being researched may have been transferred from the "Old System" to the Torrens System during the period which you are studying. In that case, you would use the land titles for the more recent period when the land would be registered under the Torrens System and an abstract for the earlier period.

Problem II: You are studying the life of a particular individual and wish to determine if he or she owned certain buildings or lands. Before attempting to use the land records, you would at least need to have the addresses of the buildings or lands in question.

If the land was registered under the Torrens System you would: (1) find the current certificate of title number for the land; (2) follow the land back to the period in which the individual under study was suspected of having owned the land (or building which is incidental to the land); (3) if that individual did in fact own the title to the land in question, his or her name would appear on the face of the title.

If the land was registered under the "Old System" you would: (1) obtain the legal description and then the abstract of title for the land in question; (2) examine the extract. If that individual did in fact own the land in question, his (her) name would appear on the abstract indicating that he (she) had received the deed for the land.

It should be noted that a land title or an abstract would not only indicate if the individual owned the land in question. It would also give an indication of that individual's financial position with respect to that land. By looking on the back of the title you can easily determine if any mortgages had been incurred while that individual held it. If you are using an abstract, any mortgages will be clearly entered.

MAPS

Soon after Manitoba entered Confederation in 1870, Dominion government land surveyors began surveying the province. Through their efforts they produced legal surveys and township diagrams which disclose historically significant information. These maps do not indicate if there were buildings present when the land was surveyed, nor do they indicate the ownership of land. The township diagrams do show where creeks once flowed, the existence of lakes, and whether land was then wooded or agricultural property. Moreover they indicate the presence of any roads or public trails which were then in existence. Thus, if you were attempting to reconstruct the Old Portage Trail, you would find the maps invaluable for the trail would be marked as a dotted line on some of the original township diagrams.

Each land titles office in Manitoba possesses the original township diagrams and legal surveys that relate to its area of responsibility. The Winnipeg office holds not only a set of maps for the region for which it is responsible, but also a duplicate set for the entire province.

LOCATION OF LAND TITLES OFFICES

There are seven land titles offices in Manitoba: in Winnipeg, Morden, Boissevain, Portage la Prairie, Brandon, Neepawa, and Dauphin. Each office is responsible for a particular Land Titles District and holds the land titles, abstract books, deeds, and maps for that particular area. Members of the legal profession and private citizens wishing to use the land titles abstract books, and deeds must pay a small charge for each document they examine.

Manitoba Directories

This list of Manitoba directories is based on Dorothy E. Ryder's "Manitoba Directories to 1950: A Preliminary Listing", *MLA Bulletin* 5:2 (1975), pp. 24-28, a bibliography compiled from the holdings of the National Library and Public Archives in Ottawa and the Archives of Saskatchewan in Regina. It has been revised, updated and expanded by Eleanor Stardom. The list has been annotated to show which directories are available at the Legislative Library in Manitoba in Winnipeg (*), at the Western Manitoba Regional Library in Brandon (**), and at the Brandon University Library (one item). Entries without these annotations are available at the above-mentioned repositories outside of Manitoba. Directories are arranged in chronological order using the following headings: (1) *Manitoba (General)*; (2) *Brandon*; (3) *Winnipeg*; (4) *Canada (General)*; (5) *Miscellaneous*; and (6) *Telephone Directories*. For a series of directories with the same title, the first issue available for examination has been used as the main entry, with the full dates of the series given below.

MANITOBA GENERAL

Manitoba directory of 1876-77 containing the names of professional and business men and other inhabitants of the province, with advertisers' classified business directory and miscellaneous directory. St. Boniface, LaRiviere and Gauvin, 1876. 162 p.*
  1877-78 — Second year*
  1878-79 — Third year*
Manitoba Kewayden and North-West Territory business directory for 1879, containing a classified business directory, an alphabetical business directory and a miscellaneous directory. Winnipeg, Times Printing and Publishing Co., 1879. 131 p.

Henderson's directory of Manitoba, with city of Winnipeg and incorporated towns of Manitoba (Emerson and Portage la Prairie) containing an alphabetical directory of the city of Winnipeg, an alphabetical directory of the residents throughout the province, a classified business directory of Manitoba, Keewatin and North-West Territory, and a miscellaneous directory for the year 1881. Winnipeg, Winnipeg Directory Publishing Co., 1881. 459 p. (Comp. James Henderson.)*

Henderson's directory of Manitoba, the city of Winnipeg and towns of Manitoba, containing an alphabetical directory of the citizens, a street directory of the city of Winnipeg, an alphabetical directory of the residents throughout the province, a classified business directory of Manitoba, Keewatin and North-West Territory and a miscellaneous directory for the year 1882. Winnipeg, Winnipeg Directory Publishing Co., 1882. 575 p.*

Henderson's Manitoba and North-West gazetteer and directory, a complete directory and gazetteer of all the towns in Manitoba and the North-West, and of all unincorporated towns, villages and settlements from Port Arthur to Silver City. The first and only gazetteer of the North-West published. Containing an alphabetical gazetteer and directory, a classified business directory and a miscellaneous directory for the year 1884. Winnipeg, Winnipeg Directory Publishing Co., 1884. 402 p.*

Henderson's Manitoba and North-Western Ontario and Northwest towns and city of Winnipeg directory. A complete directory of all the towns in Manitoba and the Northwest from Port Arthur to Silver City, also Manitoba municipalities. The only directory of the Northwest published. Containing an alphabetical directory, a classified business directory and a miscellaneous directory for the year 1886-87. Winnipeg, Winnipeg Publishing Co., 1886. 644 p.*

Henderson's Pocket Gazetteer and Traveller's Guide to all parts of Manitoba and the Northwest with complete C.P.R. Time Tables and Connecting Lines for 1887. Winnipeg. L.G. Henderson, 1887. Vol. 1, Published monthly.*

Henderson's Northwestern Ontario, Manitoba and Northwest directory and gazetteer including the city of Winnipeg. A complete directory and gazetteer of Manitoba and the Northwest, from Port Arthur to Donald, B.C., also Manitoba municipalities. The only directory of the Northwest published. Containing an alphabetical directory, a classified business directory and a miscellaneous directory for the year 1887. Winnipeg, Winnipeg Publishing Co., 1887. 757 p. (Preface: 2nd ed. Manitoba and Northwest gazetteer and directory; 8th ed. City of Winnipeg directory).*

1888 (Preface: 3rd ed. Manitoba and Northwest gazetteer and directory; 9th ed. City of Winnipeg directory)*

Henderson's gazetteer and directory of British Columbia, N.W.T., Manitoba, and Northwest Ontario, including a complete business directory of the above provinces for the year 1889. Winnipeg, Henderson Directory Co., 1889. 1109 p.*

Henderson's Manitoba, Northwest Territories and British Columbia gazetteer and directory for 1890, including a complete classified business directory. Winnipeg, Henderson Directory Co., 1890. 1169 p.*

1891*

Henderson's Manitoba and Northwest Territories gazetteer and directory for 1892, including a complete classified business directory and farmers' directory of Manitoba. Winnipeg, Henderson Directory Co., 1892. 852 p.*

1893 (v.2) — 1899 (v.8)*

Henderson's Manitoba and Northwest Territories gazetteer and directory for 1899, including a complete classified business directory and farmers' directory of Manitoba. Winnipeg, Henderson's Publishing Co. Ltd., 1899. 926, 53 p. (On cover: Vol. 21).*

Henderson's Manitoba, Northwest Territories and Western Ontario gazetteer and directory for 1900 containing a gazetteer of all cities, towns, villages, post offices, railway stations and settlements in Manitoba, Northwest Territories and western Ontario, and a complete street and alphabetical directory of Winnipeg. A complete classified business directory. Winnipeg, Henderson Publishing Co., 1900. 956 p. (On cover: v.22; Preface: 22nd ed.)*

Lovell's Directory of Manitoba and Northwest Territories for 1900-1901, including a complete classified business directory and farmers' directory of Manitoba. Winnipeg, John Lovell and Son, 1900. 1066 p. (On cover: 23rd year)*

Henderson's Manitoba, Northwest Territories and Western Ontario gazetteer and directory for 1904 including a condensed business directory of the city of Winnipeg and a complete classified business directory. Winnipeg, Henderson Directories Ltd., 1904. 691 p. (On cover: v.23)*

Henderson's Manitoba and Northwest gazetteer and directory for 1905 including Manitoba, Alberta, Saskatchewan, Western Ontario and Eastern British Columbia, and a condensed business directory of the city of Winnipeg; also a complete classified business directory of the business and professional persons appearing in all towns throughout the work. Winnipeg, Henderson Directories, 1905. 1503 p. (On cover: v.24)*

Henderson's Northwest gazetteer and directory for 1906 including Manitoba, Alberta, Saskatchewan, Athabasca, Western Ontario and Eastern British Columbia and a business directory of the city of Winnipeg with a classified business directory of the business and professional persons appearing in all towns throughout the work. Volume 25. Winnipeg, Henderson Directories, 1906. 1718 p.*

Henderson's Western Canada gazetteer and directory for 1907 including Manitoba, Alberta, Saskatchewan, Western Ontario, British Columbia, Athabasca and Yukon Territories, and business directory of the city of Winnipeg with a classified business directory of the business and professional persons appearing in all towns throughout the work. Volume 26. Winnipeg, Henderson Directories, 1907. 2571 p.*

1908 (v.27)*

Waghorn's Guide. Winnipeg, James R. Waghorn, 1884. 106 p. Issued monthly.*

Waghorn Time Table and Monthly Diary for 1885 embodying a compact business directory to Manitoba and the North-West. Winnipeg, R. Waghorn, 1885. Issued monthly.

1886-1887 2 volumes*

Waghorn's Guide and Pocket Dictionary to Manitoba and the North-West for 1888. Winnipeg, James R. Waghorn, 1888. Issued monthly.

1889-1910 22 volumes.*

Waghorn's Guide for 1911. Winnipeg, The Guide Co. Ltd., 1911. Issued monthly.

1912-1950 39 volumes.*

Directory of Northern Manitoba. 1944-1945. Regina, Overgard Directories (1946) 90 p. illus.*

BRANDON

Brandon was included in the *Henderson Manitoba* DIRECTORIES from 1882.

Brandon, Manitoba, Canada, and her industries, compiled and published by Steen and Boyce. Winnipeg, Steen and Boyce, 1882. 96 p.*

Marshallsay's directory of the city of Brandon, containing an alphabetical directory of the citizens, a street directory of the city, a classified business directory of the city, a list of real estate owners in the city, a list of farmers and real estate owners in the County of Brandon, a sketch of the rise and progress of the city, and its prominent institutions, and miscellaneous information for the year 1883. Winnipeg, Chas. A. Marshallsay & Co., 1883. 245 p.**

Brandon pocket dictionary, 1903.

v. 1? — v. 4? (Brandon University Library has 1903)

Henderson's Brandon city directory for 1907 comprising street directory of the city, an alphabetically arranged list of business firms and companies,

professional men and private citizens, and a classified business directory.
Volume 2. Winnipeg, Henderson Directories Ltd., 1907. 213 p.
1905, v. 1 — 1977 v. 51 (continuing)
(Biennial, 1905-1947). Annual 1949-   Subtitles vary)
**1909 (v. 3) - 1977 (v. 51)
 *1909 (v. 3), 1913 (v. 5), 1917 (v. 7), 1919 (v. 8), 1933 (v. 15)

WINNIPEG

Winnipeg was listed in the Manitoba directories from the first issue in 1876.
Winnipeg directory and Manitoba almanac for 1876. Postal guide and
handbook of general information. Winnipeg, Cook and Fletcher n.d.
(unpaged)
Winnipeg city directory 1883. Contains a miscellaneous directory of the city
government, police authorities, fire department, public institutions, colleges
and schools, churches, banks, secret and benevolent societies and an
alphabetically arranged list of business firms and private citizens. Also a
complete classified directory of all trades, professions and pursuits as well as a
business directory for the city of St. Boniface. Winnipeg, Steen & Boyce, 1883.
514 p.*
*Henderson's directory of the City of Winnipeg, incorporated towns of
Manitoba*, containing an alphabetical directory of the citizens, a street
directory of the city, a classified business directory of Manitoba, Keewatin
and North West Territory, and a miscellaneous directory for the year 1880.
Winnipeg: J. Henderson, 1880. 201 p. (1st edition)*
1881 (2nd ed.)*
1882 (3rd ed.)*
1883 (4th ed.)
Henderson's directory of the City of Winnipeg and the town of St. Boniface,
containing an alphabetical directory of the citizens, a street directory of the
City of Winnipeg, a subscribers' classified business directory, and a
miscellaneous directory for the year 1882. Winnipeg, Winnipeg Directory
Publishing Co., 1882. 239 p. (3rd ed.)*
1884 — 5th ed.*
1885 — 6th ed.*
1886 — 7th ed.
Henderson's directory of the City of Winnipeg, containing an alphabetical
directory of the citizens, a street directory of the City of Winnipeg, a
subscribers classified business directory, and a miscellaneous directory for the

year 1886. Winnipeg, Winnipeg Directory Publishing Co., 1886. 335 p (7th edition)*

1887 — 8th edition (Winnipeg Public Library has this and all immediately
1888 — 9th edition   following issues)
1889 — 10th edition
1890 — 11th edition
1891 — 12th edition
1892 — 13th edition
1893 — 14th edition
1894 — 15th edition
1895 — 16th edition
1896 — 17th edition

Henderson's directory of the City of Winnipeg containing an alphabetical directory of the citizens, a street directory of the City of Winnipeg, a subscribers' classified business directory, and a miscellaneous directory for the year 1888. Winnipeg, Winnipeg Directory Publishing Co., 1888. 292 p. (9th edition)*

Henderson's City of Winnipeg directory for 1896 including a complete classified business directory. Winnipeg, Henderson Directory Co., 1896. 384 + lviii p. (17th ed.)*
1899*

Henderson's City of Winnipeg directory for 1897 including a complete classified business directory. Winnipeg, Henderson Directory Co., 1897. 388 p (Preface ". . . eighteenth edition)*
1898 — 19th edition*
1899 — 20th edition

Lovell's directory of the City of Winnipeg for 1900. Winnipeg, J. Lovell and Son, 1900. 422 p.

Henderson's Winnipeg city directory for 1900 containing an alphabetical and street directory and a complete classified business directory. Winnipeg, Henderson Publishing Co., 1900. 956 p (on spine: Volume 22)
vol 23 — 1901*
vol 24 — 1902
vol 25 — 1903

Henderson's Winnipeg City Directory for 1901, containing an alphabetical and street directory and a complete classified business directory. Winnipeg, The Henderson Publishing Co. Ltd. 1901. 538 p.*
1902-1912 11 volumes*

Henderson's Winnipeg city directory for 1904 comprising a street directory of the city, an alphabetically arranged list of business firms and companies, professional men and private citizens, and a classified business directory. Winnipeg, Henderson Directories Ltd., 1904. 927 p (On spine: Volume 26)* v 27 (1905) — v 34 (1912)*

Henderson's Winnipeg city directory embracing the area of Greater Winnipeg, covering the city proper, Elmwood, St. Boniface, Norwood, St. Vital, St. James, Assiniboia and Kildonan, 1913, comprising a complete street directory of the city, an alphabetically arranged list of business firms and companies, professional men and private citizens and a classified business directory. Volume 35. Winnipeg, Henderson Directories Ltd., 1913. 1,979 p.* 1914, (v.36) — 1919, (v.41)*

Classified Business Directory 1919-1920 containing the names, addresses and phone numbers of representative manufacturing, business and professional interests of Winnipeg and vicinity. Winnipeg, The Manitoba Free Press Company Ltd., 1920. 96 p.*

Henderson's Winnipeg Directory for 1920 embracing the area of Greater Winnipeg covering the City proper, Elmwood, St. Boniface, Norwood, St. Vital, St. James, Assiniboia and Kildonan comprising a miscellaneous section and street directory of the city, an alphabetically arranged list of residents of Greater Winnipeg and a Classified Business Directory and Buyer's Guide. Winnipeg, Henderson Directories Ltd., 1920. 1,621 p. Vol. 42.* 1921 (vol. 43) to 1950 (vol. 72) (annual, 30 v.)*

CANADA (GENERAL)

McAlpine's Dominion business classified directory 1873-74, containing an alphabetical list of the names of professional and business men, manufacturers etc., in the provinces of Ontario, Quebec, Nova Scotia, New Brunswick, Newfoundland, Prince Edward Island, and Manitoba, and a general and city local miscellany. Halifax, David McAlpine, 1873. 1104p

Lovell's Canadian business guide with diary for 1886 containing classified business directory of manufacturers, wholesale merchants, insurance, railway and steamship companies etc., of the Dominion. Montreal, John Lovell, 1886. p? (Preface: ". . . second year)

Dominion of Canada Business Directory for 1890-91, comprising the provinces of British Columbia, Manitoba, Ontario, New Brunswick, Nova Scotia, Prince Edward Island and Quebec; also the North-West Territories and the colony of Newfoundland. Vol. 1 Toronto, R.L. Polk & Co., 1891. 2,805 p.*

Lovell's business and professional directory of cities and towns of Montreal, Toronto, Quebec, Hamilton, Ottawa, St. John, N.B., Halifax, London,

Winnipeg, Kingston, Victoria, Vancouver, St. Henri, Brantford, Peterboro', Charlottetown, Hull, Guelph, St. Thomas, Windsor, Sherbrooke, Belleville, Stratford, St. Catherine's, St. Cunegande, Chatham, Brockville, Moncton, Woodstock, Ont., Three Rivers, Galt, Owen Sound, Berlin, Levis, St. Hyacinthe, Cornwall, Sarnia, Sorel, New Westminster, Fredericton, Dartmouth, Yarmouth, Lindsay, Barrie, Valleyfield, Truro and Port Hope, and of all towns and banking villages in the Dominion of Canada for 1896-7. Alphabetically arranged as to places, names, business and professions. Montreal, John Lovell and Co., 1896. 1988p
Number 10
Lovell's Canadian business guide to the leading manufacturers, banks, wholesale merchants of the Dominion for 1898. Fifth issue. Montreal, John Lovell and Son, 1897. p?
Lovell's Gazetteer of the Dominion of Canada for 1908 containing the latest and most authentic descriptions of over 14,850 cities, towns, villages and places in the provinces of Ontario, Quebec, Nova Scotia, New Brunswick, Prince Edward Island, Manitoba, British Columbia, Alberta, Saskatchewan and the new districts of the North-West Territories, Yukon, Franklin, Mackenzie, Keewatin and Ungava together with Newfoundland. 4th issue. Montreal, John Lovell & Son Ltd., 1908. 970 p.*
Dominion of Canada and Colony of Newfoundland Gazetteer and Classified Business Directory for 1899 comprising the provinces of British Columbia, North-West Territories, Manitoba, Ontario, Quebec, Nova Scotia, New Brunswick, Prince Edward Island and colony of Newfoundland. Vol. II, Toronto, The Might Directory Co., 1899. 1,200 p.*
1907-08 2 volumes*
1909*
1912*
1913-15 2 volumes*
1917*
1920*
1925*
Wright's classified business and professional directory and gazetteer of the Dominion of Canada and Newfoundland, Halifax, George Wright, 1900. 981p
Tercentennial edition. Canada's manufacturers, business and professional record and gazetteer. Toronto, Trade Publishing Co., 1908. 898p
Dominion of Canada and Newfoundland gazetteer and classified business directory 1907-1908, containing classified lists of merchants, manufacturers, and professional men, Alberta, British Columbia, Manitoba, New Brunswick,

Newfoundland, Nova Scotia, Ontario, Prince Edward Island, Quebec, Saskatchewan and Yukon Territories. Toronto, Canadian Gazetteer Publishing Co., 1907. 1295 p
1909, 1912, 1914, 1915, 1917, 1919, 1920, 1922, 1923, 1925, 1926, 1927, 1929, 1930, 1931, 1933, 1935, 1938, 1940, 1942, 1944, 1946, 1947.
Canadian Parliamentary Companion for 1872 listing members of Manitoba's Executive Council, Legislative Council and Legislative Assembly with biographical sketches as well as a biographical sketch of the Lieutenant-Governor. Similar entries for the federal government. Montreal, John, Lovell, 1872. 517 p.*
1873,* 1876-80,* 1881,* 1883,* 1887,* 1889,* 1891,* 1897*
Canadian Parliamentary Guide for 1901. Ottawa, Arnott J. Magurn, 1901. 438 p.*
1903,* 1905,* 1908-1910,* 1912,* 1914,* 1915-1950*

MISCELLANEOUS

Directory of Manufacturers and Commodity Index for 1928 listing Manitoba manufacturers and an index of products made in Manitoba. Winnipeg, The Industrial Development Board of Manitoba, 1928. 128 p.*
1927-29 3 volumes*
1936*
Directory of Western Manufacturers for 1940. Winnipeg, Industrial Development Board of Manitoba, 1940. 48 p.*
1941-47 7 volumes*

WINNIPEG: MISCELLANEOUS

1. *Winnipeg, Manitoba and her Industries.* Chicago, Steen and Boyce, 1882. 131 p.*
2. *The Winnipeg Society Blue Book and Club List.* Winnipeg, Arthur L. Tunnell, 1926-27. 80 p. (illus.)*
3. *The Winnipeg Blue Book and Householder's Directory*, private address directory, Ladies' visiting and shopping guide and club lists. Winnipeg, Henderson Directories Ltd., 1907. 557 p.*

TELEPHONE DIRECTORIES

Manitoba Provincial Telephone Directory for 1921. Winnipeg, Manitoba Telephone System, 1921. 252 p.*

1927,* 1937,* 1941,* 1949*
Greater Winnipeg Telephone Directory for 1924. Winnipeg, Manitoba
Telephone System, 1924.*
1928-30 3 volumes*
1932, 1934, 1936-56 15 volumes*
Manitoba Government Telephone Directory for 1928. Winnipeg, Public
Works Department, 1928. 12 p.*
1931, 1936, 1941 plus 7 updated books prior to 1950*.

The Manitoba Telephone System, Box 6666, 41-1313 Border Street,
Winnipeg, R3C 3V6 has (1) Winnipeg directories published every six months
from 1908-1950 inclusive; (2) Manitoba directories published annually from
1908-1950 inclusive; (3) Winnipeg directories organized by telephone number
(numerical directories) published annually 1926-1950 inclusive, (stopped
publication in 1956).

Selected Archives, Libraries, and Information Services

Archives de l'Archevêché de Saint-Boniface
151, avenue de la Cathédrale, St-Boniface, Manitoba R2H 0H6

Les archives contiennent de la correspondence au sujet de l'administration du diocèse, c'est-a-dire, des lettres entre les "Fondateurs" de paroisses et les évêques. On peut y retrouver, de plus, une série complète de la revue "Les Cloches de Saint-Boniface", aide invalable au chercheur intéressé aux paroisses du diocèse de Saint-Boniface. Les régistres de paroisses (baptêmes, mariages, sépultures) demeurent dans les paroisses. Avant de consulter les archives, les chercheurs sont priés de faire un rendez-vous avec le chancelier.

The archives contain correspondence relating to the administration of the diocese, i.e. letters between the founders of various parishes and the bishop. Registers of baptisms, marriages and deaths are kept by the parishes themselves. A complete set of "Les Cloches de Saint-Boniface" is located in the archives, and could be of great value to the local historian. To consult the archives, arrangements should be made in advance with the Chancellor.

Archives of Western Canadian Legal History
Faculty of Law, Robson Hall, University of Manitoba, Winnipeg, Manitoba R3T 2N2

Holdings in the Archives of Western Canadian Legal History include: early Manitoba Bar Association and Law Society documents, early Manitoba Law School documents, legal correspondence, legal biographical and historical files, photographic collection, newspaper scrapbook collection, Winnipeg Police and Manitoba Provincial Police documents, transcript of Churchill Forest Industries Hearing, artifacts and correspondence relating to significant cases or personages, miscellaneous legal historical material.

The archives are open to the public. Not all the material may be taken out of the building. Research by appointment only.

Boissevain and Morton Regional Library
Box 340, Boissevain, Manitoba R0K 0E0

Brandon University Library
270-18th Street, Brandon University, Brandon, Manitoba R7A 6A9
The Library has 160,000 books, 1,700 newspapers and periodicals, and 75,000 government publications. Specialties include education, music, and the Public Documents Collection.

Brandon University Rural Archives
Community Resources Centre, 270-18th Street, Brandon University, Brandon, Manitoba R7A 6A9
Major holdings include: the Manitoba Pool Elevator Collection, records of 100 local Elevator Associations from 1925; the Hall Commission Records re grain handling and transportation on the prairies in 1976; a local history book collection; a newspaper collection; a collection of miscellaneous rural archival material; and a genealogical reference library.
Public access to the Archives is restricted. Researchers are advised to telephone or write in advance to arrange for an appointment.

Canadian Mennonite Brethren Archives
77 Henderson Highway, Winnipeg, Manitoba R2L 1L1
Specializing in Mennonite history and material relating to the Mennonite Brethren Church.

Canadian Pacific Archives
Windsor Station, Montreal, Quebec H3C 3E4
The archives contain minutes, financial records, correspondence, personal papers, reports, internal publications, photographs. By appointment only.

Canadian Plains Research Centre
University of Regina, Regina, Saskatchewan S4S 0A2

Conference of Mennonites in Canada (CMC) Archives
600 Shaftesbury Blvd., Winnipeg, Manitoba R3P 0M4
The Mennonite Heritage Centre is an inter-Mennonite facility housing the

records of the Conference of Mennonites in Canada, Canadian Mennonite Board of Colonization, related documents, and the personal papers of many leading persons in the Mennonite community. The extensive collection of Mennonite Genealogy, Inc., formerly of Steinbach, is now located at the Centre. Researchers are encouraged to use the facilities of the Centre, and staff researchers are available for assistance with genealogical work.

Glenbow-Alberta Institute Archives and Library Research Centre
9th Avenue and 1st Street, S.E., Calgary, Alberta T2G 0P3
   A major research centre for western Canadian history containing personal and business papers, records of societies and organizations, photographs, films, and tape recordings. The material relates mainly to Indian history and culture, history of western Canada and Arctic regions, CPR records, early records of the city of Calgary, and a comprehensive collection on ranching in southern Alberta.

Jewish Historical Society
402-365 Hargrave Street, Winnipeg, Manitoba R3B 2K3
   Archives include a pictorial collection, documents, approximately 135 oral history tapes, most of them with summary transcripts. Also included are transcripts of lectures presented at the regular meetings of the Jewish Historical Society, topics including local Jewish history and the history of the Manitoba community in general.
   Materials available on request, but appointments should be made.

Lakeland Regional Library
Box 970, Killarney, Manitoba R0K 1G0
   Brief biographies of local people.

Legislative Library
Manitoba Archives Building, 200 Vaughan Street, Winnipeg, Manitoba R3C 0P8
   Special collections include: government publications, Canadian Northwest and Manitoba history, Manitoba newspapers and local histories, political science, and public administration.

Lutheran Central Synod Archives
Lutheran Theological Seminary, 114 Seminary Crescent, Saskatoon, Saskatchewan S7N 0X3
   The archives house the records of the Central Canada Synod

(Saskatchewan, Manitoba, and Northwestern Ontario) and its predecessor bodies of the German, Swedish, and Icelandic Lutheran Churches. Materials include scattered congregational records, Synod office files concerning congregations, published anniversary booklets, and Synod newsletters with local news.

Generally, no restrictions on use of documentary items, open to the public.

Lutheran Missouri Synod Archives
Concordia Historical Institute, Department of Archives and History, The Lutheran Church — Missouri Synod, 801 De Mun Avenue, St. Louis, Missouri, U.S.A. 63105

Holdings deal with Lutheranism in North America from its earliest beginnings to the present. Of interest to the local historian would be congregational records: histories of congregations, programs of social events and biographical information on pastors and teachers.

No restrictions on public access to facilities aside from those imposed upon certain materials by their donors. Membership in the Institute is encouraged but not required for use of facilities. Some resources may be used only within the Institute, others may be sent out on loan. Genealogical research or queries on specific and general historical matters will be handled by the staff for a fee.

Manitoba Department of Agriculture Library
Call the Department of Agriculture, listed under the Government of Manitoba in the Winnipeg telephone directory.

Holdings include 1600 books, 180 periodicals, and 6000 government publications specializing in agriculture. Limited public access.

Manitoba Department of the Attorney General, Winnipeg Land Titles Office
Call the Department of the Attorney General, listed under the Government of Manitoba in the Winnipeg telephone directory.

Manitoba Department of Cultural Affairs and Historical Resources
Call the department, listed in the Winnipeg telephone directory under Government of Manitoba.

Responsible for the identification, preservation and interpretation of provincial heritage resources through its history, archaeology and architectural history sections. Public enquires are welcome.

Manitoba Department of Health and Social Development, Office of Vital Statistics
104 Norquay Building, Winnipeg, Manitoba R3C 0P8
The province has recorded and preserved registrations of birth, stillbirth, death and marriage since 1882 under governmental authority. Some church records for various denominations dating back to 1812 are also preserved. Records are confidential. Certificates are restricted and issued to persons concerned provided that proper information and fee are given at the time of application. Genealogical searches are done for a fee of $5.00. Applicants must provide required information and proof of kinship or written permission from next of kin.

Manitoba Department of Natural Resources, Crown Lands Section
Call the department, listed under the Government of Manitoba in the Winnipeg telephone directory.
Files include township records, records of early land transactions. Some very old files from the Department of the Interior, referring to parish lots, have been microfilmed. No restrictions on use of files, but availability of working space is limited.

Manitoba Department of Public Works, Design Service
Call the department, listed in the Winnipeg telephone directory under Government of Manitoba.
The department keeps on file drawings of most governmental buildings, although some may be incomplete and others not originals. Researchers should contact the department to ascertain whether the required information is available. Original tracings may not be removed from the office but prints can be made.

Manitoba Historical Society
Room M211, 190 Rupert Avenue, Winnipeg, Manitoba R3B 0N2
The Manitoba Historical Society library contains a number of local histories, as well as the complete set of transactions of the Historical and Scientific Society of Manitoba, and the *Manitoba Pageant*.

Manitoba Genealogical Society
P.O. Box 2066, Winnipeg, Manitoba R3C 3R4

Manitoba Telephone System
Box 6666, 41-1313 Border Street, Winnipeg, Manitoba R3C 3Y6
The library contains all Winnipeg and provincial telephone directories

from the first published in 1908 to the present, as well as copies of the Numerical Telephone Directory issued from 1926 to 1956.

The library is open to the public, but books are not allowed out of the building.

Mohyla Institute Archives
1240 Temperance Street, Saskatoon, Saskatchewan S7N 0P1
Ukrainian historical materials. By appointment only.

Oblate Archives
Archives Deschatelets, 175 rue Main, Ottawa, Ontario K1S 1C3
Archives historiques des Oblats du Canada, microfilms, photographies, manuscrits. By appointment only.

Provincial Archives of Alberta
12845-102nd Avenue, Edmonton, Alberta T5N 0M6
Contains records of the provincial government, religious archives and collections of maps, photographs, films, audio tapes and private papers relating to the province of Alberta.

Provincial Archives of British Columbia
655 Belleville Street, Victoria, British Columbia V8V 1X4
Manuscripts and government records, private papers, books, newspapers, visual records, maps relating to the history of British Columbia. Notable holdings include a Northwest collection and an extensive photography collection.

Provincial Archives of Manitoba
Manitoba Archives Building, 200 Vaughan Street, Winnipeg, Manitoba R3C 0P8
Contains manuscript, map and picture collections, and public records relating to the history of Manitoba. Major collections include: records of the government of Assiniboia 1835-1869, records of the government of Manitoba from 1870, Archives of the Hudson's Bay Company from 1671; records of the Anglican Ecclesiastical Province of Rupert's Land and Diocese of Rupert's Land, fur trade collection, papers and correspondence of Louis Riel, and papers of premiers and cabinet ministers.

Provincial Archives of Saskatchewan
(Regina Office), University of Regina, Regina, Saskatchewan S4S 0A2

(Saskatoon Office), University of Saskatchewan, Saskatoon S7N 0N0
Both offices contain records of the provincial government and government of the North-West Territories, Saskatchewan homestead records of the old Department of the Interior, newspaper collections, private papers, maps and photographs pertaining to the province of Saskatchewan.

Public Archives of Canada
395 Wellington Street, Ottawa, Ontario K1A 0N3
Government records, manuscripts, photographs, maps, drawings, paintings, prints, films and sound recordings, machine readable records.

Public Library Services
139 Hamelin Street, Winnipeg R3T 4H4
Houses an extensive collection of local histories that can be consulted through the interlibrary loan service by those individuals residing in centres with a public library and through direct mail service by individuals residing in centres without public library facilities. Also publishes a newsletter that informs the public library community of newly published Manitoba local histories.

Reimer Historical Library and Archives
Mennonite Village Museum, Steinbach, Manitoba.

Research Centre for Ethnic Studies
University of Calgary, 2920-24th Avenue, N.W., Calgary, Alberta T2N 1N4

Richardson Securities of Canada Research Library
One Lombard Place, Winnipeg, Manitoba R3B 0X2
Company research only.

Royal Canadian Mounted Police Museum
P.O. Box 6500, Regina, Saskatchewan S4P 3S7

Société Historique de Saint-Boniface, La
B.P. 125, Saint-Boniface, Manitoba R2H 3B4
Les archives et la bibliothèque de la Société sont logés à présent au troisième étage du Collége universitaire de Saint-Boniface, 200, avenue de la Cathédrale. On y retrouve les matériaux suivants: environ 1200 dossiers classés sous "personnes", "lieux" et "sujets" ce qui comprend des institutions et des organisations, des coupures des presse, d'intérêt géréral et particulier, une collection de photos, de la documentation caratographique non-classé, une collection de journaux franco-manitobains ainsi que l'Opinion Publique — Hebdo de Montréal, la

"Collection Riel", — qui comprend des documents originaux, la "Collection Champagne" — qui traite surtout des La Vérendrye et du Régime Francais, la "Collection Piction" — généalogie, correspondance et papiers, et autres collections speciales: D'Eschambault, Trudel, Goyette, Bernard, Frémont, Benoist, Selkirk, le Collège de Saint-Boniface et la Société Franco-Manitobaine ainsi que l'Association d'Education des Canadiens-francais de l'Ouest, les recensements et registres de Saint-Boniface, quelque 5000 volumes, tous d'une manière ou d'une autre portant sur le Manitoba et son passé,

Les chercheurs doivent faire un rendez-vous pour consulter les documents de la Société. Certaines collections ne sont pas accessibles au publique, selon la demande des donateurs.

The library and archives, presently housed on the third floor of le Collège universitaire de Saint-Boniface, 200, avenue de la Cathèdrale, contains the following: about 1200 files, classified under "persons", "localities" and "subjects" — including institutions and organizations, newspaper clippings of general and special interest, a photographic collection, unclassified map collection, newspaper collection including French-language Manitoba newspapers and "L'Opinion Publique" (a Montreal weekly), several collections including the "Riel Collection" with original documents, the "Champagne Collection" (chiefly relating to La Vérendrye and the early French Régime), as well as recent history, the "Picton Collection" (genealogy, papers and correspondence) and other special collections: D'Eschambault, Trudel, Goyette, Bernard, Selkirk, Frémont, Collège de Saint-Boniface, Benoist, la Société Franco-Manitobaine and l'Association d'Education des Canadiens Francais de Manitoba, Saint Boniface registers and census returns, and about 5000 volumes relating to Manitoba and its past.

Researchers must make an appointment to consult the archives. Certain collections are not open to the public, at the request of the donors.

Ukrainian Catholic Church Consistory
St. Vladimir and Olga Cathedral, 115 McGregor Street, Winnipeg, Manitoba R2W 4V6

The archives contain marriage, baptism and death records in Ukrainian, Latin and English, as well as many books in the Ukrainian language. Open to the public.

Ukrainian Cultural and Educational Centre
184 Alexander Avenue, E., Winnipeg, Manitoba R3B 0L6
Holdings include 20,000 books, 500 bound periodicals and 100

periodicals specializing in the fields of Ukrainian history, language, literature and art.

Ukrainian Greek Orthodox Church Consistory
9 St. John's Avenue, Winnipeg, Manitoba R2W 1G8
    Parish records are contained in these archives, but they are not available to the general public. Arrangements are being made to have archival materials microfilmed and copies sent to the National Library. For copies of baptism, marriage and death certificates, researchers should write or telephone and copies will be mailed.

University of Manitoba: Elizabeth Dafoe Library
University of Manitoba, Winnipeg, Manitoba R3T 2N2
    The library houses over one million books, periodicals, government publications and a wide variety of maps, microfilm and microfiche items. Special collections include Icelandic and Slavic documents and books.

University of Manitoba Archives
Elizabeth Dafoe Library, University of Manitoba, Winnipeg, Manitoba R3T 2N2
    Special collections include the papers of J.W. Dafoe, Ralph Connor, and Frederick Philip Grove, as well as the Dysart Memorial Collection of Rare Books and Manuscripts.

University of Winnipeg: Manitoba Conference Archives of the United Church of Canada
Manitoba Conference Archives, Rare Book Room — Library, University of Winnipeg, 515 Portage Avenue, Winnipeg, Manitoba R3B 2E9
    Holdings include the administrative records, including some records and registers of marriage, baptisms and burials, of the Methodist, Presbyterian and Congregational Churches in Manitoba from 1870 to 1925, and the United Church in Manitoba from 1925 to the present. At present there are no restricted holdings.

University of Winnipeg Library
515 Portage Avenue, University of Winnipeg, Winnipeg, Manitoba R3B 2E9
    The library houses 300,000 books and periodicals and a variety of newspapers, pamphlets and microfilm items. Special collections include Anthropology, Canadiana, Local Histories, Theology and Government documents.

Western Canadian Aviation Museum
11 Lily Street, Winnipeg, Manitoba (mailing address: Box 99, Station C, Winnipeg, Manitoba R3M 3S6)

Bibliography

In order that the bibliography may serve as a quick reference guide to those readers pursuing specific themes, it has been organized to conform as closely as possible with the chapter arrangement of the *Guide*. It should be noted that this is a selected bibliography, one which lists only the most useful works on each subject. If further information is required on a particular subject, refer to the general bibliographies listed in section I below, or to the bibliographies in standard works.

GENERAL REFERENCE WORKS

Bibliographies

Artibise, Alan F. J. *Western Canada Since 1870: A Select Bibliography and Guide.* Vancouver: University of British Columbia Press, 1978.

Fowke, Edith, C. Henderson and J. Brooks. *A Bibliography of Canadian Folklore in English.* Downsview: York University, 1976.

Granatstein, J. L., and Paul Stevens (eds.). *Canada Since 1867: A Bibliographical Guide.* 3rd ed.: Toronto: Hakkert, 1977.

Heggie, Grace F. *Canadian Political Parties, 1867-1968: A Historical Bibliography.* Toronto: Macmillan, 1977.

Historic Resources Branch, Government of Manitoba. The branch has commissioned several specialized bibliographies, including "Women," Artists," "Hudson Bay Lowlands," "Red and Assiniboine."

Historical and Scientific Society of Manitoba. *Local History in Manitoba; a key to places, districts, schools and transport routes.* Winnipeg: Historical and Scientific Society of Manitoba, 1976.

Morley, Marjorie, comp. *A Bibliography of Manitoba from Holdings in the Legislative Library of Manitoba.* Winnipeg: Legislative Library, 1970.

Peel, Bruce Braden. *A Bibliography of the Prairie Provinces to 1953.* 2nd ed. Toronto: University of Toronto Press, 1973.

Thibault, Claude. *Bibliographia Canadiana.* Toronto : Longman, 1973.

Approaches to Manitoba History

Donnelly, M. S. *The Government of Manitoba.* Toronto: University of Toronto Press, 1963.

Historical and Scientific Society of Manitoba. *Transactions.* (Many volumes of essays which have been published at various times from the 1880s to the present.

Jackson, James A. *Centennial History of Manitoba.*

Loveridge, D. M. "The Rural Municipality of Sifton." M.A. thesis, University of Manitoba, 1977.

Morton, William L. *Manitoba: A History.* Toronto: University of Toronto Press, 1957, 1967.

Potyondi, Barry S. "Country Town: The History of Minnedosa, Manitoba, 1879-1922," M.A. thesis, 1978, University of Manitoba.

Warkentin, J. H. and R. I. Ruggles, eds. *Manitoba Historical Atlas.* Winnipeg: Manitoba Historical Society, 1970.

Weir, T. R., ed. *Economic Atlas of Manitoba.* Winnipeg: Department of Industry and Commerce, 1960.

To Local Historians in Manitoba

Baum, Willa K. *Oral History for the Local Historical Society.* Nashville: American Association for State and Local History, n.d.

Burcaw, G. Ellis. *Introduction to Museum Work.* Nashville: American Association for State and Local History, n.d.

Creigh, Dorothy Weyer. *A Primer for Local Historical Societies.* Nashville: American Association for State and Local History, 1976.

Dempsey, Hugh A. *How to Prepare a Local History.* Calgary: Glenbow Alberta Institute, 1969.

Frank H. Epp. *Stories With Meaning: A Guide for the Writing of Congregational Histories.* (Waterloo, Ont.: Mennonite Historical Society of Canada, 1978).

Felt, Thomas E. *Researching, Writing and Publishing Local History.* Nashville: American Association for State and Local History, 1976.

Guldbeck, Per E. *The Care of Historical Collections: A Conservation Handbook for the Nonspecialist.* Nashville: American Association for State and Local History, n.d.

Guthe, Carl E. *The Management of Small History Museums*. Nashville: American Association for State and Local History, n.d.

Neal, Arminta. *Exhibits for the Small Museum: A Handbook*. Nashville: American Association for State and Local History, n.d.

Silvestro, Clement M. *Organizing a Local Historical Society*. Nashville: American Association for State and Local History, n.d.

Weinstein, Robert A. and Larry Booth. *Collection, Use, and Care of Historical Photographs*. Nashville: American Association for State and Local History, n.d.

To the Teacher

Acton, Janice, et al., eds. "How to do Research." *Women at Work, Ontario, 1850-1930*. Toronto: Canadian Women's Educational Press, 1974.

Douch, Robert. *Local History and the Teacher*. London: Routledge and Kegan Paul, 1967.

Ekwall, E. *Concise Oxford Dictionary of Place Names*, (1960 edition).

Fahrni, M., and W. L. Morton. *Third Crossing: A History of the First Quarter-Century of the Town and District of Gladstone, Manitoba*. Winnipeg: 1946.

Finberg, H. P. R., and V. H. T. Skipp. *Local History: Objective and Pursuit*. 2nd ed.: Newton Abbott: David and Charles, 1973.

Fredrickson, Mary. *Local Studies*. Halifax: Atlantic Institute of Education, 1977. (This booklet is well worth buying.)

_____. "From the Outside Looking In: The Museum as a Local Studies Resource." *Proceedings of the Annual Conference of the Canadian Museums Association*, 1974.

Hamilton, William B. *Local History in Atlantic Canada*. Toronto: Macmillan, 1974.

_____. "Structuring a Program in Local History." *The History and Social Science Teacher* X:2 (Winter 1974).

Milligan, J. "Proposal for a Course in 'Local History'." *Social Studies Review*, Nova Scotia Teachers Union, 4:8 (September, 1973), 3-12.

Rudnychyj, J. B. *Manitoba Mosaic of Place Names*. Winnipeg: Trident Press, 1970.

Stevenson, H. A., and F. H. Armstrong, eds. *Approaches to Teaching Local History, Using Upper Canadian and Ontario Examples*. Toronto: Oxford University Press, 1969.

Trask, Deborah, and Betty Ann Milligan. *A Cemetery Survey: Teachers' Manual*. Halifax: Nova Scotia Museum, n.d.

Wedlake, W. "A Study in Local Geography: Analyzing a Town", Student Guide issued by the Manitoba Social Science Teachers Association.

American Association for State and Local History: Technical Leaflets

These publications may be obtained at nominal cost from the American Association for State and Local History, 1400 Eighth Avenue South, Nashville, Tennesee 37203.

Museum Exhibits
Preparing Your Exhibits: Methods, Materials, and Bibliography
Displaying Your Costumes: Some Effective Techniques
Preparing Your Exhibits: Case Arrangement and Design
Constructing Modular Furniture for Exhibit Mock-Ups
Exhibit Planning: Ordering Your Artifacts Interpretively
The Exhibit of Documents: Preparation, Matting, and Display Techniques

Audio-Visual Programs
Tape-Recording Local History
Producing the Slide Show for Your Historical Society

Publications
Publishing in the Historical Society
Reaching the Public: The Historical Society Newsletter
Making and Correcting Copy for Your Printer
Phototypesetting: Getting the Most for Your Money.

Administering Your Collection
Storing Your Collections: Problems and Solutions
Collecting Historical Artifacts: An Aid for Small Museums
Documenting Collections: Museum Registration and Records
Historical Society Records: Guidelines for a Protection Program
Filing Your Photographs: Some Basic Procedures
Cataloging Photographs: A Procedure for Small Museums
Data Retrieval Without a Computer
Converting Loans to Gifts: One Solution to "Permanent" Loans

Historical and Genealogical Research
Writing Local History: The Use of Social Statistics
Cemetery Transcribing: Preparations and Procedures

Genealogical Research: A Basic Guide
Methods of Research for the Amateur Historian
Indexing Local Newspapers
Local History Manuscripts: Sources, Uses, and Preservation

Local History Perspectives
The Role of Local History, by James C. Olson
The Evaluation of Historic Photographs, by Paul Vanderbilt

Historical Societies and Programs
Planning Tours for Your Historical Society
Recruiting Members for Your Historical Society
The Library in the Small Historical Society
History for Young People: Projects and Activities
A Guide to Planning Local History Institutes
History for Young People: Organizing a Junior Society
Insuring Against Loss
Securing Grant Support: Effective Planning and Preparation
Planning a Local Museum: An Approach for Historical Societies
Using Consultants Effectively
Planning Museum Tours: For School Groups
Historical Markers: Planning Local Programs
Financing Your History Organization: Setting Goals
Maps in the Small Historical Society: Care and Cataloging
Using Oral History for a Family Project
Working Effectively with the Press: A Guide for Historical Societies

THE ENVIRONMENT

General Works

Smith, P. J., ed. *The Prairie Provinces*. Studies in Canadian Geography published for the 22nd International Geographical Congress. Toronto: University of Toronto Press, 1972.
Warkentin, John, ed. *Canada: A Geographical Interpretation*. Toronto and London: Methuen, 1968.

Cartography

British Museum. *Catalogue of Printed Charts and Plans*. 15 Vols. London: British Museum, 1967.

The National Atlas of Canada. 4 Editions (1906, 1915, 1957, 1974) Ottawa: Department of Energy, Mines and Resources and Information Canada, 1974.
Public Archives of Canada. *Catalogue of the National Map Collection.* 16 Vols. Boston, 1976. (Manitoba localities are listed under the numbers 500-599 and, for pre-1870 material, 700-799.).

Soils

Ellis, J. H. *The Land for Thine Inheritance.* Winnipeg: Manitoba Department of Agriculture, revised edition 1947.
Ellis, J. H. *The Soils of Manitoba.* Winnipeg: Economic Survey Board, 1938.
Faculty of Agriculture and Home Economics, University of Manitoba. *Principles and Practices of Commercial Farming.* Winnipeg: University of Manitoba, Fifth ed., 1977.

Resources

Canada, Department of Agriculture, Economics Branch. *Prairie Regional Studies in Economic Geography.* Ottawa: Department of Agriculture, 1968 — (six volumes on Manitoba).
Manitoba Economic Survey Board. *Reports.* (22 Vols, 1938-39).
Murchie, R. W., and H. C. Grant. *Unused Lands of Manitoba.* Winnipeg: Minister of Agriculture and Immigration, 1926.
Weir, T. R., ed. *Economic Atlas of Manitoba.* Winnipeg: Department of Industry and Commerce, 1960.

Climate

Canada Department of Marine and Fisheries. *Reports on the Meteorological, Magnetic and other observations . . . .* Ottawa: Department of Marine and Fisheries, 1870-1890: 1895-1915.
_____. *Monthly Record of Meteorological Observations.* Toronto: Department of Marine and Fisheries, 1916- present.
   (These two series, available at the Legislative Library, contain records from an increasing number of weather stations in the province [10 in 1890, 68 in 1960], for such daily and monthly and seasonal topics as temperature, relative humidity, precipitation, cloud, and so on. Summaries of climatic data appear in the Meteorological Branch reports from time to time, as in the 1965 and 1968 volumes.)
Connor, A. J. *The Climate of Manitoba.* Winnipeg: Economic Survey Board, 1939.

Laycock, Arleigh. *Water Deficiency and Surplus Patterns in the Prairie Provinces*. Regina: n.p. n.d.
_____. *Water Deficiency Patterns in the Prairie Provinces*. Prairie Province Water Board, Report No. 8, 1964.
Longley, Richard W. *The Climate of the Prairie Provinces*. Ottawa: Information Canada, 1972.
_____. *et al. Bibliography of Climatology for the Prairie Provinces*, 1957-1969. Edmonton. University of Alberta Press, 1971.

Surveying and Topography

Sebert, L. M. *Every Square Inch: The Story of Canadian Topographic Mapping*. Ottawa: Department of Energy, Mines and Resources, Surveys and Mapping Branch, 1970.
_____. "The Three Mile Sectional Maps of the Canadian West." *The Cartograper*, 4:2 (December 1967), 112-119.
_____. "The History of the Rectangular Township of the Canadian Prairies." *The Canadian Surveyor*, XVII:5 (December 1963), 380-389.
(See also section on land and settlement)

Flora

Harrison, J. D. B. *The Forests of Manitoba*. Ottawa: Department of the Interior, Forest Service Bulletin No. 85, 1934.
Scoggan, H. J. *The Flora of Manitoba*. Ottawa: National Museum of Canada Bulletin No. 140, Biological Series No. 47, 1957.
Watts, F. B. "The Natural Vegetation of the Southern Great Plains of Canada." *Geographical Bulletin*, 14 (1960), 25-43.

Geology

Davies, J. F., et al. *Geological and Natural Resources of Manitoba*. Winnipeg: Manitoba Department of Mines and Natural Resources, 1962.
Johnston, A. G. *Index of Publications of the Geological Survey of Canada, 1845-1958*. Department of Mines and Technical Surveys, 1961.
Wallace, R. C. *The Geological Formations of Manitoba*. Winnipeg: Natural History Society of Manitoba, 1925.

Hydrography

Canada Department of Marine and Fisheries. Hydrographic charts are available
for a number of Manitoba areas, including the coast of Hudson Bay and Lake
Winnipeg.

POPULATION STUDIES

Davidson, C. B. *The Population of Manitoba*. Winnipeg: Economic Survey
Board, 1938.
Manitoba Department of Industry and Commerce. *Regional Analysis Program:
Southern Manitoba*. Carvalho-Page Group, program advisers. Winnipeg, 1972.
With an update, 1975 (2 vols.).
Urquhart, M. C., and K. A. H. Buckley, eds. *Historical Statistics of Canada*.
Toronto: Macmillan, 1965.
Warkentin, John. "Western Canada in 1886." *Historical and Scientific Society of
Manitoba Papers*, Series III, No. 20 (1963-64), 85-116.
_____. "Manitoba Settlement Patterns." *Historical and Scientific Society of
Manitoba Transactions*, Series III, No. 16 (1959-60), 62-77.
Weir, Thomas R. "Pioneer Settlement in the Southwest Manitoba." *Canadian
Geographer*, VIII:2 (1964), 64-71.
_____. "Settlement in Southwest Manitoba 1870-1891." *Historical and Scien-
tific Society of Manitoba Transactions*, Series III, No. 17 (1960-61), 54-64/

TRANSPORTATION AND COMMUNICATIONS

General Works

Dillabough, J. V. *Transportation in Manitoba*. Winnipeg: Economic Survey
Board, 1938.
Glazebrook, G. P. de T. *A History of Transportation in Canada*. Toronto: Ryerson,
1938.

Fur Trade Troutes

Alcock, F. J. "Past and Present Trade Routes." *The Geographical Review*, X
(1920), 57-83.
Morse, Eric W. *Fur Trade Canoe Routes of Canada/Then and Now*. Ottawa:
Queen's Printer, 1969.
Voorhis, Ernest (comp.). *Historic Forts and Trading Posts of the French Regime*

and of the English Fur Trading Companies. Ottawa: Department of the Interior, 1930.

Trails and Roads

Brehaut, H. B. "The Red River Cart and Trails: The Fur Trade." *Historical and Scientific Society of Manitoba Transactions,* Series III, No. 28 (1971-72), 5-36.

Klassen, Henry C. "The Red River Settlement and the St. Paul Route, 1859-1870." M.A. thesis, University of Manitoba, 1963.

Nute, Grace Lee. "The Red River Trails." *Minnesota History Bulletin,* 6:3 (September 1925), 278-282.

Potyondi, B. "The Boundary Commission Trail." A paper prepared for The Historic Resources Branch, Manitoba Department of Tourism, Recreation and Cultural Affairs, 1976.

Robertson, W. G. "History of the Trans-Canada Highway." *Canadian Good Roads Association, Proceedings of the 25th Annual Convention,* 1940, 213-223.

Russell, R. C. *The Carlton Trail.* Saskatoon: Prairie Books, 1971.

Water Transportation

Anonymous. "The Merchant Marine of Manitoba: A List of Vessels and Registered Tonnage Plying Red River and Lake Winnipeg." *The Dominion* (July 1912), 244.

McFadden, Molly. "Assiniboine Steamboats." *Beaver,* Outfit 284 (June 1953), 38-42.

_____. "Steamboats on the Red." *Beaver,* Outfit 281 (June 1950), 31-33, (Part 1); (September 1950), 25-29, (Part 2).

Railways

Bladen, M. L. *Construction of Railways in Canada to the Year 1885.* Contributions to Canadian Economics, Volume 5. Toronto: University of Toronto Press, 1932.

Bladen, M. L. *Construction of Railways in Canada from 1885 to 1931.* Contributions to Canadian Economics, Volume 7. Toronto: University of Toronto Press, 1934.

Dorman, Robert, comp. *A Statutory History of the Steam and Electric Railways of Canada, 1836-1937.* Ottawa: King's Printer, 1938.

Earl, L. F. "The Hudson Bay Railway." *Historical and Scientific Society of Manitoba Transactions*, Series III, No. 14 (1957-58), 24-32.

Fleming, Howard A. *Canada's Arctic Outlet: A History of the Hudson Bay Railway.* Berkeley: University of California Press, 1957.

Innis, H. A. *A History of the Canadian Pacific Railway.* London: P. S. King, 1923.

Lamb, W. Kaye. *History of the Canadian Pacific Railway.* New York: Macmillan, 1976.

Letourneau, Roger. "Manitoba's Railways: A Pilot Study of the Historical Reources of Manitoba." Prepared for The Historic Resources Branch, Manitoba Department of Tourism, Recreation, and Cultural Affairs, 1974.

Moore, George A. "Manitoba's Railways." Parts I and II. *Canadian Rail* 282 (1975) and 285 (1975).

McDougall, J. Lorne. *Canadian Pacific: A Brief History.* Montreal: McGill University Press, 1968.

Regehr, T. D. *The Canadian Northern Railway: Pioneer Road of the Northern Prairies 1895-1918.* Toronto: Macmillan of Canada and Maclean-Hunter Press, 1976.

Stevens, G. R. *History of the Canadian National Railways.* New York: Macmillan, 1973.

_____. *Canadian National Railways.* 2 Vols.: Toronto: Clarke Irwin, 1960, 1962.

Postal Service, Telegraph and Telephone

Campbell, Murray. "The Postal History of Red River, British North America." *Historical and Scientific Society of Manitoba Transactions*, Series III, No. 6 (1951), 7-19.

Loveridge, D. M. *A Historical Directory of Manitoba Newspapers, 1859-1978.* Winnipeg: University of Manitoba Press, 1980.

Muir, Gilbert A. "A History of the Telephone in Manitoba." *Historical and Scientific Society of Manitoba Transactions*, Series III, No. 21 (1964-65), 69-82.

Warkentin, John. "Western Canada in 1886." *Historical and Scientific Society of Manitoba Transactions*, Series III.

Aviation

Ashley, Charles A. *The First Twenty-Five Years: A Study of Trans-Canada Airlines.* Toronto: Macmillan, 1963.

Brown, Roy. "The Origin and Growth of Western Canadian Aviation." *Historical and Scientific Society of Manitoba Transactions*, Series III, No. 14 (1957-58), 54-60.

AGRICULTURE

General Works

Britnell, G. E., and V. C. Fowke. *Canadian Agriculture in War and Peace, 1935-50.* Stanford: Stanford University Press, 1962.

Ellis, J. H. *The Ministry of Agriculture in Manitoba, 1870-1970.* Winnipeg: Manitoba Department of Agriculture, 1971.

Forsythe, J. E. *History of Manitoba Agricultural Extension Staff 1913-70.* Winnipeg: The Author, 1974.

Fowke, Vernon C. *The National Policy and the Wheat Economy.* Toronto: University of Toronto Press, 1957. Reprint 1971.

_____. *Canadian Agricultural Policy: The Historical Pattern.* Toronto: University of Toronto Press, 1946. Reprint 1971.

MacEwan, J. W. G. *Harvest of Bread.* Saskatoon: Prairie Books, 1969.

McKilligan, W. C. "An Outline of the History of Agriculture in Manitoba." A paper given before the Historical and Scientific Society of Manitoba at Winnipeg, 6 November 1929.

MacPherson, Ian. *Each For All: A History of the Co-operative Movement in English Canada.* Toronto: Macmillan, 1979.

Morton, W. L. "Agriculture in the Red River Colony." *Canadian Historical Review,* 30:4 (December 1949), 305-321.

Murray, S. N. *The Valley Comes of Age: A History of Agriculture in the Valley of the Red River of the North, 1812-1920.* Fargo: North Dakota Institute for Regional Studies, 1967.

Regina, University of. *Development of Agriculture on the Prairies: Proceedings of Seminar.* Regina, 1975.

Strange, H. G. L. *A Short History of Prairie Agriculture.* Winnipeg: Searle Grain Company, 1954.

Thompson, John H. *The Harvest of War: The Prairie West, 1914-1918.* Toronto: McClelland and Stewart, 1978.

The Grain Trade and Government Policy

Drummond, William M., W. J. Anderson and T. C. Kerr. *A Review of Agricultural Policy in Canada.* Ottawa: Agriculture Economics Research Council, 1966.

Garland, S.W., and S. C. Hudson. *Government Involvement in Agriculture: a report prepared for the Federal Task Force on Agriculture.* Ottawa: Queen's Printer, 1969.

MacGibbon, D. A. *The Canadian Grain Trade, 1931-1951.* Toronto: University of Toronto Press, 1952.

_____. *The Canadian Grain Trade*. Toronto: Macmillan, 1932.

Piper, Clarence. *Principles of the Grain Trade of Western Canada*. Winnipeg: Empire Elevator Company, 1915.

Wilson, C. F. *A Century of Canadian Grain: Government Policy to 1951*. Saskatoon: Western Producer Prairie Books, 1978.

Agricultural Cooperation and Farm Movements

Colquette, R. D. *The First Fifty Years: A History of United Grain Growers Limited*. Winnipeg: Public Press, 1957.

Hamilton, F. W. *Service at Cost: A History of Manitoba Pool Elevators, 1925-1975*. Saskatoon: Modern Press, 1975.

Mackintosh, W. A. *Agricultural Cooperation in Western Canada*. Toronto: Ryerson, 1924.

McCutcheon, B. "The Patrons of Industry in Manitoba, 1890-1898." *Historical and Scientific Society of Manitoba Transactions*, Series III, No. 22 (1965-66), 7-25.

_____. "The Economic and Social Structure of Political Agrarianism in Manitoba, 1870-1900." Ph.D. thesis, University of British Columbia, 1974.

Michell, H. "The Cooperative Store in Canada." *Queen's Quarterly*, XXIII:3 (1916), 317-338.

Morton, W. L. *The Progressive Party in Canada*. Toronto: University of Toronto Press, 1950.

Panting, G. E. "A Study of the United Farmers of Manitoba to 1928." M.A. thesis, University of Manitoba, 1954.

Patton, Harald S. *Grain Growers' Cooperation in Western Canada*. Cambridge: Harvard University Press, 1928.

Sharp, Paul F. *The Agrarian Revolt in Western Canada*. Minneapolis: University of Minnesota Press, 1948.

Wood, Louis A. *A History of Farmers' Movements in Canada*. 1924. Reprint, Toronto: University of Toronto Press, 1975.

Science and Technology

Livestock

Bell, J. R., et al. *The Livestock Industry of Manitoba*. Winnipeg: Economic Survey Board, 1939.

MacEwan, J. W. G., and A. H. MacEwan. *The Science and Practice of Canadian Animal Husbandry*. Toronto: T. Nelson, 1936.

Crops
Alberta Wheat Pool. *The Story of Wheat*. Calgary: The Alberta Wheat Pool, 1940.
Buller, A. H. R. *Essays on Wheat*. New York: Macmillan, 1919.
Spector, David. *Field Agriculture in the Canadian Prairie West 1870-1940 with emphasis on the period 1870-1920*. Ottawa: Parks Canada, Manuscript Report No. 205, 1977.
Swanson, W. W., and P. C. Armstrong. *Wheat*. Toronto: Macmillan, 1930.

Exhibitions
MacEwan, J. W. G. *Agriculture on Parade: The Story of the Fairs and Exhibitions of Western Canada*. Toronto: T. Nelson, 1950.

Machinery
MacEwan, J. W. G. *Power for Prairie Plows*. Saskatoon: Western Producer Book Service, 1974.
Peck, John A. *Farm Machinery in Perspective*. Saskatoon: Modern Press, 1965.
Symes, O. "Agricultural Technology and Changing Life on the Prairies." In *Proceedings of Seminar: Development of Agriculture on the Prairies*. Regina: University of Regina, 1975, 35-44.
Vicas, Alex. G. "Research and Development in the Farm Machinery Industry." Study Report No. 7. Canada. Royal Commission on Farm Machinery. Ottawa: Queen's Printer, 1970.

BUSINESS AND LABOUR

Bibliographies

Brown, Barbara E. (ed.), *Canadian Business and Economics: A Guide to Sources of Information/Sources d'informations economiques commerciales canadiennes*. Ottawa: Canadian Library Association, 1976.
Canadian Bankers' Association. *A Bibliography of Canadian Banking/Une bibliographie sur la banque au Canada*. Toronto: Canadian Bankers' Association, 1971.

General Works

Bercuson, David. *Confrontation at Winnipeg: Labour, Industrial Relations and the General Strike*. Montreal: McGill-Queen's University Press, 1974.
Cheasley, C. H. *The Chain Store Movement in Canada*. Orillia: McGill University Economic Studies, No. 17, 1930.

Dawson, C. A., and Eva R. Younge. *Pioneering in the Prairie Provinces: The Social Side of the Settlement Process.* Toronto: Macmillan, 1940.

Innis, H. A. "Industrialism and Settlement in Western Canada." *Report of the International Geographical Congress,* Cambridge, July 1928, 369-376.

Kerr, Donald. "Wholesale Trade on the Canadian Plains in the Late Nineteenth Century: Winnipeg and its Competition." In Howard Palmer (ed.), *The Settlement of the West.* Calgary: Comprint Publishing, 1977.

Macpherson, Ian. "The Co-operative Union of Canada and the Prairies." In Susan M. Trofimenkoff (ed.), *The Twenties in Western Canada.* Ottawa: National Museum of Man, 1972.

McCormack, A. Ross. *Reformers, Rebels, and Revolutionaries: The Western Canadian Radical Movement, 1899-1919.* Toronto: University of Toronto Press, 1977.

PROVINCIAL AND FEDERAL POLITICS

Beck, J. Murray. *Pendulum of Power: Canada's Federal Elections.* Scarborough: Prentice-Hall, 1968.

Clark, W. L. R. "Politics in Brandon City, 1899-1946." Ph.D. thesis, University of Alberta, 1976.

Cook, Ramsay. *The Politics of John W. Dafoe and the Free Press.* Toronto: University of Toronto Press, 1963.

Donnelly, Murray S. *The Government of Manitoba.* Toronto: University of Toronto Press, 1963.

Fisk, Larry J. "Controversy on the Prairies: Issues in the General Provincial Elections of Manitoba, 1870-1969." Ph.D. thesis, University of Alberta, 1975.

Jackson, James A. *The Centennial History of Manitoba.* Toronto: McCelland and Stewart for the Manitoba Historical Society, 1970.

Johnson, J. K., ed. *The Canadian Directory of Parliament, 1867-1967.* Ottawa: Public Archives of Canada, 1968.

Kendle, John. *John Bracken.* Toronto: University of Toronto Press, 1979.

McNaught, K. *A Prophet in Politics: A Biography of J. S. Woodsworth.* Toronto: University of Toronto Press, 1959.

Morton, W. L. *Manitoba: A History.* Toronto: University of Toronto Press, 1957; 2nd ed. 1967.

_____. *The Progressive Party in Canada.* Toronto: University of Toronto Press, 1950.

Peterson, T. E. "Manitoba." In Martin Robin (ed.), *Canadian Provincial Politics.* Scarborough: Prentice-Hall, 1972.

Stanley, G. F. G. *The Birth of Western Canada: A History of the Riel Rebellions.* 1936. Reprint, Toronto: University of Toronto Press, 1961.
Young, Walter D. *The Anatomy of a Party: The National C.C.F. 1932-1961.* Toronto: University of Toronto Press, 1969.

LOCAL GOVERNMENT

Bibliographies

Canadian Council on Urban and Regional Research. *Urban and Regional References, 1945-69/Références urbaines et régionales, 1945-69.* Ottawa: Canadian Council on Urban and Regional Research, 1971 (with an annual supplement).
Grasham, W. E., comp. *Canadian Public Administration Bibliography/Administration publique canadienne: bibliographie.* Toronto: Institute of Public Administration of Canada, 1972.

General Works

Donnelly, Murray S. "Manitoba: A Case Study in Canadian Provincial and Local Government." Lectures presented at University College, University of Manitoba, Winnipeg, April 1965.
_____. *The Government of Manitoba.* Toronto: University of Toronto Press, 1963.
Ewart, Alan C. "The Municipal History of Manitoba." In S. Morley Wickett (ed.), *Municipal Government in Canada,* Vol. II, Toronto: University of Toronto Press, 1907.
Fisher, Murray. "Local Government Reorganization." *Historical and Scientific Society of Manitoba Transactions,* Series III, No. 17 (1961), 15-23.
Phillips, A. F. "The Development of Municipal Institutions in Manitoba to 1886." M.A. thesis, University of Manitoba, 1948.
Rowat, Donald C. *Your Local Government.* 2nd ed. Toronto: Macmillan, 1975.

SOCIAL STUDIES

Fowke, Edith. "Songs of a Manitoba Family." *Canadian Folk Music Journal,* 3 (1975).
Mills, G. E., and D. W. Holdsworth. *The B.C. Mills Prefabricated System: The Emergence of Ready-Made Buildings in Western Canada.* Canadian Historic Sties, Occasional Papers in Archaeology and History, No. 14, Ottawa, 1976.

Klymasz, R. B. *Folk Narrative among Ukrainian Canadians in Western Canada.* Ottawa: National Museum of Man, 1975.

Miller, Carolynn L. "Genealogical Research: A Basic Guide." *History News,* 24:3 (March 1969). (Also available as Technical Leaflet 14, American Association for State and Local History, 1315-8th Avenue South, Nashville, Tennessee, 37203.)

Peacock, Kenneth. *A Survey of Ethnic Folk Music across Western Canada.* Ottawa: National Museum of Man, 1963.

_____. *Twenty Ethnic Songs from Western Canada.* Ottawa: National Museum of Man, 1966.

McCracken, Jane, et al. *Oral History: Basic Techniques.* Winnipeg: Manitoba Museum of Man and Nature, 1974.

Moir, G., et al. *Early Buildings of Manitoba.* Winnipeg: Peguis, 1973.

National Museums of Canada. *Catalogue of Sales Publications.*

Samuel, Raphael. "Local History and oral History." *History Workshop,* I (1976), 191-208.

EDUCATION

Crunican, Paul. *Priests and Politicians: Manitoba Schools and the Election of 1896.* Toronto and Buffalo: University of Toronto Press, 1974.

Perfect, Mary. "One Hundred Years of Rural Schools in Manitoba: A Brief History of their Establishment, Re-organization and Dissolution, 1871-1971." M.Ed. thesis, University of Manitoba, 1977.

Shanks, D., and K. Wilson. *Educational Journal of Western Canada 1899-1903: Introduction and Index.* Winnipeg: Manitoba Educational Research Council, 1976.

_____. *The Western School Journal 1906-1938: Introduction and Index.* 2 vols. Winnipeg: Faculty of Education, University of Manitoba, 1976.

Wilson, Keith. "The Development of Education in Manitoba." Ph.D. thesis, Michigan State University, 1967.

Woods, D. S. *Education in Manitoba.* 2 vols. Winnipeg: Economic Survey Board 1938.

RELIGION

Allen, Richard. *The Social Passion: Religion and Social Reform in Canada, 1914-28.* Toronto: University of Toronto Press, 1971.

_____. ed. *Religion and Society in the Prairie West.* Regina: Canadian Plains Research Centre, 1974.

_____. ed. *The Social Gospel in Canada*. Ottawa: National Museum of Man, 1975.

McLaurin, C. C. *Pioneering in Western Canada: A Story of the Baptists*. Calgary: The author, 1939.

Moir, John. *Enduring Witness: A History of the Presbyterian Church in Canada*. Toronto: Presbyterian Publications, 1974.

Morice, A. G. *The Catholic Church in Western Canada*. Winnipeg: Canadian Publishers, 1931.

Boon, T. C. B. *The Anglican Church from the Bay to the Rockies: A History of the Ecclesiastical Province of Rupert's Land and its dioceses from 1820 to 1950*. Toronto: Ryerson, 1962.

Brooks, William Howard. "Methodism in the Canadian West in the Nineteenth Century." Ph.D. thesis, University of Manitoba, 1972.

Emery, George N. "Methodism on the Canadian Prairies, 1896-1914: The Dynamics of an Institution in a New Environment." Ph.D. thesis, University of British Columbia, 1970.

Oliver, E. H. *The Winning of the Frontier: A Study in the Religious History of Canada*. Toronto: United Church Publishing House, 1930.

Thompson, M. E. *The Baptist Story in Western Canada*. Calgary: Baptist Union of Western Canada, 1974.

Trosky, O. S. *The Ukrainian Greek Orthodox Church in Canada*. Winnipeg: Bulman Bros., 1968.

OTHER ACTIVITIES: LAW

Gibson, Dale, and Lee. *Substantial Justice: Law and Lawyers in Manitoba, 1670-1970*. Winnipeg: Peguis Publishers, 1972.

McLeod, R. C. *The NWMP and Law Enforcement 1873-1905*. Toronto: University of Toronto Press, 1976.

Oliver, E. H. *The Canadian North-West: Its Early Development and Legislative Records*. 2 vols. Ottawa: Publications of the Canadian Archives, No. 9, 1914.

Smith, George. "Early Police in Manitoba." Unpublished manuscript, Manitoba Historical Society.

Stubbs, Roy St. George. *Four Recorders of Rupert's Land*. Winnipeg: Peguis Publishers, 1967.

Williams, E. H. "Aspects of the Legal History of Manitoba." *Historical and Scientific Society of Manitoba Transactions*, Series III, No. 4 (1948), 48-61.

SPECIAL THEMES IN MANITOBA HISTORICAL STUDIES

Archaeology

Hlady, Walter, ed. *Ten Thousand Years: Archaeology in Manitoba.* Winnipeg: Manitoba Archaeological Society, 1970.

Single-Enterprise Communities

Elias, P.D. *Metropolis and Hinterland in Northern Manitoba.* Winnipeg: Manitoba Museum of Man and Nature, 1975.
Emberley, G. C. (comp.). *Highlights of Settlement History: Northern Manitoba.* Winnipeg: Planning and Priorities Committee, 1971.
Hunter, B. F. C. "The Development of New Manitoba, 1912-1930." M.A. thesis, University of Western Ontario, 1974.
Lucas, Rex A. *Minetown, Milltown, Railtown: Life in Canadian Communities of Single Industry.* Toronto: University of Toronto Press, 1971.
Manitoba Department of Northern Affairs. *Community Profiles.* Winnipeg, 1975. (This series includes several volumes on each northern area.)
_____. *Let's Talk About Local Government in Northern Communities.* Winnipeg, 1973.
Morton, W. L. *Northern Manitoba.* Unpublished typescript for the Government of Manitoba, 1950. (Available for consultation at the Legislative Library.)
Rothney, Russell. "Mercantile Capital and the Livelihood of Residents of the Hudson Bay Region: A Marxist Interpretation." M.A. thesis, University of Manitoba, 1975.

Native Studies

Abler, T.S., et al. *A Canadian Indian Bibliography 1960-1970.* Toronto: University of Toronto Press, 1974.
Camponi, L., and W. Oppen, comps. *Indian Reserve Maps in the National Map Collection,* Vol. I *Western Canada.* Ottawa, Public Archives of Canada, 1979.
Canada. *Statement of the Government of Canada on Indian Policy, 1969.* Ottawa: Supply and Services, Department of Indian Affairs and Northern Development, 1969.
Giraud, Marcel. *Le Métis Canadien: Son Role dans l'histoire des provinces de l'ouest.* Paris: Institut d'Ethnologie, 1945.
Harper, Allan G. "Canada's Indian Administration: Basic Concepts and Objectives." *America Indigena,* V:2 (April 1945), 119-132.

Hawthorn, Harry B. (ed.) *A Survey of the Contemporary Indians of Canada; a report on economic, political and educational needs and policies.* (Ottawa: Indian Affairs Branch, Department of Indian Affairs and Northern Development, 1966-68) 2 Vols.

Hlady, Walter. "Indian Migrations in Manitoba and the West." *Historical and Scientific Society of Manitoba Transactions,* Series III, No. 17 (1960-61), 24-53.

Indian Treaties and Surrenders from 1680 to 1890. Ottawa: King's Printer, Vols. 1 and 2, 1905; vol. 3, 1912.

Jenness, Diamond. *The Indians of Canada.* Ottawa: National Museum, 1932.

Lagassé, Jean H. *A Study of the Population of Indian Ancestry Living in Manitoba.* 3 vols. Winnipeg: Department of Agriculture and Immigration, Social and Economic Research Office, 1959.

MacInnis, T. R. L. "History of Indian Administration in Canada." *Canadian Journal of Economics and Political Science,* XII:3 (August 1946), 387-394.

Manitoba Department of Education. *Resource Materials: Native Peoples of Manitoba.* Winnipeg: Native Education Branch, 1976.

Morris, Alexander. *The Treaties of Canada with the Indians of Manitoba and the North-West Territories, including the negotiations on which they were based, and other information relating thereto.* 1880, Reprint, Toronto: Coles Publishing, 1971.

Patterson, E. Palmer. *The Canadian Indian: A History Since 1500.* Don Mills: Collier-Macmillan, 1972.

Ray, Arthur J. *Indians in the Fur Trade.* Toronto: University of Toronto Press, 1974.

Rich, E. E. *The Fur Trade and the Northwest to 1857.* Toronto: McClelland and Stewart, 1967.

Vickers, Chris. "Aboriginal Backgrounds in Southern Manitoba." *Historical and Scientific Society of Manitoba Transactions,* Series III, No. 2 (1946), 3-9.

Ethnic Studies

Chiel, Arthur A. *The Jews in Manitoba: A Social History.* Toronto: University of Toronto Press for the Manitoba Historical Society, 1961.

Comeault, Gilbert-Louis. "The Politics of the Manitoba School Question and Its Impact on L.-P.-A. Langevin's Relations with Manitoba's Catholic Minority Groups, 1895-1915." M.A. thesis, University of Manitoba, 1979.

Dawson, C. A. *Group Settlement: Ethnic Communities in Western Canada.* Toronto: Macmillan, 1936.

Dorge, Lionel (ed.). *Introduction a l'étude des Franco-Manitobains: Essai his-*

torique et bibliographique. St. Boniface: La Société Historique de Saint-Boniface, 1973.

Francis, E. K. *In Search of Utopia: The Mennonites in Manitoba*. Glencoe: Free Press, 1955.

Gregorovich, A. (comp.). *Canadian Ethnic Groups Bibliography*. Toronto: Ontario Department of Provincial Secretary and Citizenship, 1972.

Houser, George J. *The Swedish Community at Eriksdale*. Ottawa: Canadian Centre for Folk Culture Studies, National Museum of Man.

Kristjanson, W. *The Icelandic People in Manitoba: A Manitoba Saga*. Winnipeg: The Author, 1965.

Marunchak, Michael H. *The Ukrainian Canadians: A History*. Ottawa: Ukrainian Free Academy of Sciences, 1970.

Painchaud, Robert. "The Catholic Church and the Movement of Francophones to the Canadian Prairies," Ph.D. thesis, University of Ottawa, 1976.

Peters, Victor. *All Things Common: The Hutterian Way of Life*. 1965 Reprint, New York: Harper Torchbooks, 1971.

Sharp, Emmitt F., and G. Albert Kristjanson. *The People of Manitoba*. Winnipeg: Manitoba Department of Agriculture and Conservation, 1965.

Sutyla, C. "Multicultural Studies in Canada." *Communique: Canadian Studies*, 3:1. (October 1976). Association of Canadian Community Colleges, 1750 Finch Avenue East, Willowdale, OIntario. (Other bibliographical guides are published in this series.)

Turek, Wiktor. *Poles in Manitoba*. Toronto: Polish Research Institute in Canada, Studies 5, 1967.

Wilson, Keith, and James B. Wyndels. *The Belgians in Manitoba*. Winnipeg: Peguis Publishers, 1976.

Woodsworth, J. S. *Strangers Within Our Gates*. 1909. Reprint, Toronto: University of Toronto Press, 1972.

Yuzyk, Paul. *The Ukrainians in Manitoba: A Social History*. Toronto: University of Toronto Press, 1953.

Urban Studies: Winnipeg and Brandon

Artibise, Alan, F. J. *Winnipeg: an Illustrated History*. Toronto: James Lorimer and National Museum of Man, 1977.

_____. *Winnipeg: A Social History of Urban Growth, 1874-1914*. Montreal: McGill-Queen's University Press, 1975.

_____ and E. H. Dahl. *Winnipeg in Maps/Winnipeg par les Cartes, 1816-1972*. Ottawa: Public Archives of Canada, 1975.

Rea, J. E. *Parties and Power: An Analysis of Winnipeg City Council, 1919-1975*.

Appendix IV. Committee of Review City of Winnipeg Act. Winnipeg: Manitoba Department of Urban Affairs, 1976.

Sloane, D. L., J. M. Roseneder and M. J. Hernandez, eds. *Winnipeg: A Centennial Bibliography.* Winnipeg: Manitoba Library Association, 1974.

Weir, Thomas R., comp. and ed. With the assistance of Ngok-Wai Lai. *Atlas of Winnipeg.* Toronto: University of Toronto Press, 1978.

Wichern, P. H., ed. *The Development of Urban Government in the Winnipeg Area* and *Studies in Winnipeg Politics.* Vols. I and II. Winnipeg: Manitoba Department of Urban Affairs, 1975, 1976.

WRITING A BOOK ON LOCAL HISTORY IN MANITOBA

Hill, Mary, and Wendell Cochran. *Into Print: A Practical Guide to Writing, Illustrating, and Publishing.* Los Altos, Calif.: William Kaufmann, Inc.

APPENDIX 1: LAND AND SETTLEMENT RECORDS

Friesen, J. "Expansion of Settlement in Manitoba: 1870-1900." *Historical and Scientific Society of Manitoba Transactions,* Series III, No. 20 (1963-64), 35-48.

Galbraith, J. S. "Land Policies of the Hudson's Bay Company, 1870-1913." *Canadian Historical Review,* XXXII:I (March 1951), 1-21.

Hedges, J. B. *Building the Canadian West: The Land and Colonization Policies of the Canadian Pacific Railway.* New York and Toronto: Macmillan, 1939.

_____. *The Federal Railway Land Subsidy Policy of Canada.* Cambridge: Harvard University Press, 1934.

Martin, Chester. *"Dominion Lands" Policy.* Edited by L. H. Thomas. 1938. Reprint, Toronto: McClelland and Stewart, 1973.

Morton, A. S. *History of Prairie Settlement.* Toronto: Macmillan, 1938.

Pridham, E. A. "The Title to land in Manitoba." *Historical and Scientific Society of Manitoba Transactions,* Series III, No. 13 (1956-57), 7-26.

Richtik, James M. "Manitoba Settlement: 1870 to 1886." Ph.D. dissertation, University of Minnesota, 1971.

Thomson, Donald W. *Men and Meridians: The History of Surveying and Mapping in Canada.* 3 Vols. Ottawa: Queen's Printer, 1967.

Tyman, John L. *By Section, Township and Range: Studies in Prairie Settlement.* Brandon: Assiniboine Historical Society, 1972.

_____. "Prairie Settlement: The Legislative Framework." In A. H. Paul and E. H. Dale (eds.), *Southern Prairies: Background Papers.* Regina: University of Saskatchewan, 1972.